RESEARCH REPORT JANUARY 2015

# School Closings in Chicago
Understanding Families' Choices and Constraints for New School Enrollment

Marisa de la Torre, Molly F. Gordon, Paul Moore, and Jennifer Cowhy
with Sanja Jagešić and Michelle Hanh Huynh

## TABLE OF CONTENTS

**1** Executive Summary

**5** Introduction

*Chapter 1*
**7** Overview of School Closings Process

*Chapter 2*
**15** Enrollment Patterns After Schools Closed

*Chapter 3*
**23** Understanding Enrollment Patterns after Schools Closed

*Chapter 4*
**35** Interpretive Summary

**39** References

**41** Appendices A-C

## ACKNOWLEDGEMENTS

The authors gratefully acknowledge the Spencer Foundation for its support, which made this study possible. We would also like to acknowledge the support of the Chicago Public Schools for providing us the administrative data that allowed us to do this work. We thank our Steering Committee members for their thoughtful comments, especially Luisiana Meléndez, Veronica Anderson, and John Barker for doing a close read of the report. As always, colleagues from the University of Chicago Consortium on Chicago School Research have given us so much encouragement and feedback during the course of this work. We especially thank Penny Bender Sebring, Elaine Allensworth, Sue Sporte, Jenny Nagaoka, Josh Klugman, and David Johnson for their insightful feedback. Special thanks to research assistants Catherine Alvarez-McCurdy and Kiara Nerenberg for their help with different tasks, as well as Eliza Moeller and Kaleen Healey for expertise as technical readers. We were fortunate to receive substantial feedback and assistance from the communications team: Emily Krone, Bronwyn McDaniel, and Jessica Puller.

Finally, and most important, we thank the families that took part in this study and shared their experiences and thoughts with us. We sincerely hope they see their experiences reflected in these pages.

We also gratefully acknowledge the Spencer Foundation and the Lewis-Sebring Family Foundation, whose operating grants support the work of UChicago CCSR.

---

This report was produced by UChicago CCSR's publications and communications staff: Emily Krone, Director for Outreach and Communication; Bronwyn McDaniel, Senior Manager for Outreach and Communication; and Jessica Puller, Communications Specialist.

Graphic Design: Jeff Hall Design
Photography: Lloyd DeGrane, David Schalliol
Editing: Ann Lindner

---

01.2015/pdf/jh.design@rcn.com

# Executive Summary

Confronted with significant financial challenges and declining student enrollment, many urban districts are resorting to closing schools as a way to consolidate resources among fewer schools. Facing similar challenges, the Chicago Board of Education voted in May 2013 to close 47 underutilized elementary schools—at the time, the largest number of schools closed in one year by any district in the nation.[1]

Closing schools is difficult and often fiercely contested. Schools are one of the few stable institutions in some communities, and closing them has the potential to further destabilize fragile neighborhoods and disproportionately affect the most vulnerable students in the system. Districts must weigh the impact that closing schools has on those directly affected with any benefits that might accrue from consolidating resources into fewer school buildings. When districts decide to close schools, they are often met with strong resistance from families, community groups, and school staff. In Chicago, the closings were concentrated in depopulated neighborhoods in the South and West sides—neighborhoods already grappling with very high levels of poverty, crime, and unemployment. Because of the vulnerability of the affected students, critics of the Chicago Public Schools (CPS) policy worried that displaced students would end up in poor educational environments and suffer both emotionally and academically.

In an attempt to address some of these concerns, CPS assigned all displaced students to a *"welcoming school"* that was rated higher-performing than their closed schools. The district made investments in these welcoming schools and expanded the already existing Safe Passage program to include routes to these schools with adult monitors. Although the district assigned students to specific higher-rated welcoming schools, given the open enrollment system in Chicago, families could enroll their children in any other school in the district with open seats.

CPS's policy, in part, was a response to prior research on school closings, which found that only students who attended substantially higher-performing schools had better academic outcomes; yet, only a small portion of displaced students from these past closings attended substantially higher-performing schools.[2]

As other districts look to shape closing policies that will at once save money and optimize student learning, it is imperative to understand whether CPS's policy ultimately succeeded in sending students to higher-performing schools. Likewise, it is crucial to understand why students ultimately enrolled in the schools they did—whether higher- or lower-performing. Our mixed-methods study addresses these questions by examining where students from closed schools enrolled the following fall and investigating why students did or did not enroll in higher-rated schools as the district intended. Affecting nearly 12,000 students, Chicago's decision to

---

1   The Board of Education voted to close 49 schools, but two of them had a closing date later than June 2013. The decision also included closing a high school program in an elementary school. CPS labels a school as underutilized if the enrollment of the school is below 80 percent of its capacity.

2   de la Torre & Gwynne (2009); Engberg et al. (2012).

close 47 schools provides a unique opportunity to study not only the policy itself but also the mechanisms that facilitate or constrain families from enrolling their children in higher-rated schools.

Data for the quantitative section of this report come from CPS administrative records on all students who attended schools that were closed, including information on demographics, enrollment, test scores, neighborhood crime reports from the Chicago Police Department, and data on neighborhoods from the U.S. Census. Qualitative data come from interviews with 95 families directly affected by school closings. The report focuses on students who were enrolled in grades K-7 in May 2013 and had to reenroll in a new elementary school the following year.

Below we describe the findings using the quantitative data and on page 3 we describe the findings from the qualitative interviews.

## What Are the Characteristics of the Students Affected by School Closures?

**Schools that were closed were serving a larger share of vulnerable students than other schools in CPS.** Students affected by school closures were more likely to receive free or reduced-price lunch, receive special education services, and be old for their grade. Their families were also more likely to have changed residences in the year prior to the school closings. Eighty-eight percent of students affected by school closures were African American. All the elementary schools that were initially targeted for closure (underutilized and low-performing) served similarly vulnerable students.

## Where Did Displaced Students Enroll the Following Fall?

**Nearly all displaced students (93 percent) attended schools with higher performance ratings than the closed schools.** However, almost one-quarter of students attended schools that were lower-rated than their designated welcoming schools.

**Among those students who reenrolled in a CPS school, 66 percent attended their designated welcoming school.** This rate varied greatly from one closed school to another, ranging from 6 percent in some schools to 90 percent in others. One-quarter of students enrolled into traditional elementary schools other than their assigned welcoming school, 4 percent found seats in charter schools, and 4 percent enrolled into magnet schools. Besides the 48 designated welcoming schools, the students enrolled in 311 other CPS schools across the city. Families were more likely to attend their designated welcoming school if they lived in close proximity to it. Our analysis also showed a positive relationship between designated welcoming schools' safety rating on the 2013 My Voice, My School survey and the likelihood of families attending those schools.[3] They also were more likely to attend the designated welcoming school if it was relocated to the site of the closed school. Surprisingly, students assigned to higher-rated welcoming schools were less likely to attend those schools than students assigned lower-rated welcoming schools.

**Students who enrolled in other CPS schools often chose a school with a lower performance policy rating than the designated welcoming school.** Students who lived in neighborhoods with few high-rated schools were more likely to attend schools on probation if they did not enroll in their designated welcoming school. Of the students who attended other CPS schools in the fall with a performance policy rating, 64 percent attended a school with lower points than the designated welcoming school.[4] Even though, in most cases, those welcoming schools had higher performance policy points than the closed schools, 22 percent of students who did not enroll in designated welcoming schools attended a school with lower performance policy points than their closed school.

**There was no increase in the number of families that left CPS after schools closed.** Following the school closures, 94 percent of students enrolled in CPS schools with 6 percent leaving the district; this rate is similar to prior years.

---

3  My Voice, My School is an annual survey of learning conditions taken by students and teachers in Chicago Public Schools.

4  Schools do not have a performance policy rating if they have not been in operation for long and, therefore, there is not enough data for the district to calculate the rating.

## Why Did Families Enroll Their Children into Designated Welcoming Schools?

**Many families we interviewed chose to enroll their children into their designated welcoming school because the school matched their priorities and needs.** These families said they chose to enroll their children into their designated welcoming school mainly because the school was close to home, they believed the school had strong academics, and/or they had personal connections like friends and staff from closed schools who transferred into the welcoming school.

**Some families believed they had no other choice but to enroll their child(ren) into the designated welcoming school.** Some families, based on the information they received or heard, believed they had to enroll their children into the designated welcoming school. The district automatically enrolled students into the designated welcoming schools by mid-June. Many families believed that because of this automatic enrollment, they could not choose a different school.

**Some families faced constraints or barriers getting into other schools across the district that limited their options.** Some families enrolled in the designated welcoming school because they could not get into other schools to which they applied. Other families said they felt the welcoming school was their only option because of practical constraints. Among the reasons cited were neighborhood safety concerns, lack of access to affordable transportation, the schools not having the necessary supports and/or services for children with individualized education programs (IEPs), not having any other options in the neighborhood, and not having enough time to explore other school options.

## Why Did Families Enroll Their Children into Other CPS Schools?

**Some families faced barriers enrolling into their designated welcoming school.** Families that moved out of or did not live in attendance area boundaries of the closed schools were particularly affected. Some families were turned away from enrolling into the district designated welcoming schools because their addresses fell outside of the attendance area boundaries. Other families said they moved or lived too far away from the welcoming school and/or could not afford transportation to get their children to the welcoming schools.

**Some families chose not to enroll their children in the designated welcoming school because it did not match the criteria they were looking for in schools.** Families that enrolled their children into other higher-rated schools did so because they prioritized academic quality over other factors. The primary reason these families rejected their designated welcoming school was because they perceived it to be of lower academic quality. These interviewees also mentioned some safety concerns with their designated welcoming school, heard negative things about the school from families and friends, or said they did not want to send their children to a school that was on previous potential closings lists.

**Proximity to home was the primary reason families enrolled their children in lower-rated schools instead of a designated welcoming school.** The deciding factor for families that enrolled in a lower-rated school, other than their designated welcoming school, was the school's close proximity to their home. These parents also wanted schools that met their children's academic needs, although distance was prioritized over other considerations, oftentimes because of safety concerns. Finding a school close to home was not only about convenience and safety but also about families' practical circumstances and realities. Parents and guardians worried about being able to get children to and from school when the weather was bad or when their children got sick, for example.

**For many families, academic quality meant something different than a schools' performance policy rating.** The way many parents defined academic quality was different from the official markers of quality represented by the district's performance policy rating system. For example, for many families academic quality meant having after-school programs, certain curricula and courses, small class sizes, positive and welcoming school environments, and/or one-on-one attention from teachers in classes. Although some families did talk about their school's official policy rating, most factored in these other "unofficial" indicators of academic quality when making their school choice decisions.

# Introduction

Many urban districts across the nation are dealing with declining enrollments and budgetary deficits. In response, some districts are opting to close a number of their low-enrollment schools in order to consolidate resources and save money.[5]

In addition to budgetary and enrollment concerns, the surge in school closings comes amidst federal calls to shutter chronically under-performing schools. U.S. Secretary of Education Arne Duncan listed closing schools as one of the Race to the Top models for turning around low-performing schools.[6] Chicago is one of the districts that have initiated several previous rounds of school closings, citing both low-performance and underutilization.

Faced with a reported $1 billion deficit, the Chicago Board of Education voted in May 2013 to close 47 underutilized elementary schools. At the time, it was the largest mass school closing in the nation's history.[7] CPS officials acknowledged how difficult this would be for families, but stated it was necessary due to fiscal constraints and declining student enrollment in schools located in some of the city's depopulating neighborhoods. According to district officials there were 403,000 students enrolled in CPS, which had seats for 511,000—a disparity that created a *"utilization crisis"* in which sparse resources were spread too thin across too many schools with low enrollment.[8]

The mass closings were met with fierce resistance from many families, neighborhood groups, and the Chicago Teachers Union. Families worried about children's safety because students would now have further to travel to their new schools, oftentimes through unfamiliar and, in some cases, unsafe areas of gang activity. Other groups questioned, among other things, the formula used to determine whether a school was underutilized and whether the schools receiving displaced students were high performing enough to really improve students' educational outlook.

One of the most contentious aspects of the policy was that the schools proposed for closure were primarily concentrated in the city's South and West sides, in depopulating neighborhoods struggling with high levels of crime and poverty. Critics feared that the closings would create more instability in the lives of children and families who were already among the district's most vulnerable. Because of this vulnerability, critics worried that these displaced students would be particularly likely to end up in poor educational environments and suffer both emotionally and academically.

---

5  Detroit, Philadelphia, Washington, DC, Memphis, and St. Louis are among those districts facing these challenges and closing schools.
6  Duncan (2009).
7  The Board of Education voted to close 49 schools, but two of them had a closing date later than June 2013. The decision also included the closure of a high school program in an elementary school. CPS labels a school as underutilized if the enrollment of the school is below 80 percent of its capacity.
8  Chicago Public Schools (2013, January 28).

In an attempt to address some of these concerns, CPS assigned all displaced students to a *"welcoming school"* that was rated higher-performing than their closed schools. CPS CEO Barbara Byrd-Bennett stated, *"By consolidating these schools, we can focus on safely getting every child into a better performing school close to their home."* [9] As the quote suggests, the district factored in not only performance but also distance and student safety when assigning welcoming schools. The district assigned welcoming schools that were within one mile of the school that closed and put resources into Safe Passage routes to provide students a safe walk to and from school. In addition, they made investments that could be used toward enhancements such as air conditioning, science labs, and new programs.

Implicit within the district's policy rhetoric are two distinct underlying assumptions. The first is that if students attend higher-performing schools, they will, in fact, perform better academically. CPS's policy, in part, was a response to prior research on school closings, which found that only students who attended substantially higher-performing schools had better academic outcomes; yet, only a small portion of displaced students from past closings attended substantially higher-performing schools.[10]

The second underlying assumption is that families would choose to send their children to the better-performing welcoming schools to which they were assigned, where the district would invest resources, add new programs, and create Safe Passage routes. However, families may have had different criteria for determining which school would best serve their children and they may not have seen welcoming schools as good options. They also may have faced specific barriers or constraints unknown to the district that led them to enroll in certain schools rather than others. Prior research does not tell us why students who were displaced by past school closings enrolled in the schools they did—why didn't more students attend better performing schools? Our mixed-methods study aims to bridge that gap by answering the following primary research questions:

## Where did students from the closed schools enroll the following fall?

- Did families leave CPS at higher rates than in the past?
- To what extent did families enroll in the assigned welcoming schools?
- If families chose other schools, to what extent did they end up in higher-performing or lower-performing schools?

## Why did families enroll in designated welcoming schools or opt to enroll in other schools in the district?

- Why did families end up in higher- or lower-performing schools than the schools CPS assigned to them?
- What barriers did families face in deciding on a new school?

As other districts look to shape closing policies that will at once save money and optimize student learning, it is imperative to understand whether CPS's policy ultimately succeeded in sending students to higher-performing schools. Likewise, it is crucial to understand why students ultimately enrolled in the schools they did—whether higher- or lower-performing. Affecting nearly 12,000 students, Chicago's decision to close 47 schools provides a unique opportunity to study not only the policy itself but also the mechanisms that facilitate or constrain families from enrolling their children in higher-rated schools.

Chapter 1 outlines key elements of the school closing policy. Chapter 2 examines where students from closed schools enrolled the following fall and the characteristics of these schools using administrative data. Chapter 3 uses interviews with families affected by this round of school closings to understand why families enrolled their children where they did. Chapter 4 concludes with some implications of our findings.

---

**9** Chicago Public Schools (2013, March 20).

**10** de la Torre & Gwynne (2009); Engberg et al. (2012).

CHAPTER 1

# Overview of School Closings Process

On May 22, 2013, the Chicago Board of Education voted to close 47 underutilized elementary schools at the end of the 2012-13 academic year. Earlier in the school year, CPS announced that a total of 330 schools were under-enrolled and at-risk for closure. Throughout the year, the district pared down the number under consideration for closure until the final vote took place.[11] In March, with the announcement of 54 elementary schools slated for closure, the district outlined plans for the transition and identified which schools would be receiving the displaced students. In this chapter, we describe different aspects of the policy and the process CPS outlined for transitioning students into designated welcoming schools. **See the box entitled** *"Timeline Around School Closures Process and Related Events"* for more details.

CPS cited many different factors when selecting which schools to close; among them were enrollment, performance measures, and the overall condition of the school buildings. The final closures list was comprised of schools with utilization rates below 70 percent, fewer than 600 students, and not in the process of adding grade levels. These were schools that did not recently experience a significant school action and were not the top-rated schools in the district, meaning that their accountability rating was below *"excellent standing"* (Level 1) and not on an upward trajectory.[12] Other factors listed were the characteristics of the other elementary schools in the area.

Each closed school was paired with one or more designated welcoming school(s) that were higher-performing, based on the 2012-13 performance policy rating **(see box entitled** *"CPS Performance Policy"*). In some cases, the district chose welcoming schools that had received the same performance rating level as the closed school, but were higher-rated on the majority of the performance policy metrics.[13] In addition, these welcoming schools had to have enough available seats to enroll the displaced students and be located within one mile of the closing school. Forty-eight schools were designated as welcoming schools, with some of the schools associated with more than one closed school. **See Table A.1 in Appendix A** for a list of closed schools, their designated welcoming schools, and the characteristics of each.

---

[11] In December 2012, the district announced that 330 schools were underutilized. By February 2013, the district named 129 elementary schools among those 330 that were still under consideration for closure. By the end of March 2013, a more definitive list of 54 schools was announced. The school board voted to close 47 elementary schools and one high school program by the end of that year and to phase out two more elementary schools within two years. Four schools were withdrawn from the list.

[12] CPS identified schools that experienced a significant school action as those that were designated welcoming schools in the past three years or were part of a co-location in the 2012-13 academic year. Chicago Public Schools (2013a, March 21).

[13] The *2012-2013 Guidelines for school actions* outlines in detail what the district determined to be higher-performing schools. Chicago Public Schools (2012).

# Timeline Around School Closures Process and Related Events

| | About School Closings | Related Events |
|---|---|---|
| **October 2012** | Barbara Byrd-Bennett is named the Chief Executive Officer of the Chicago Public Schools (CPS).[A]<br><br>CPS releases draft guidelines that will be used to determine decisions around school closures, consolidations, reassignment boundary changes, phase-outs, and co-locations. The public has 21 days to provide feedback on the draft guidelines.[B] | |
| **November 2012** | An independent Commission on School Utilization is formed to lead community engagement, gather information from the public, and provide a written report to guide CPS in making recommendations around school closures. The commission starts a series of six public hearings.[C]<br><br>CPS is granted an extension until March 31 to announce all proposed school actions to be taken at the end of the current academic year. Under current law, the deadline for that announcement is on December 1.[D] | |
| **December 2012** | CPS releases a list identifying 330 schools that are underutilized, according to enrollment figures from September 2012.[E]<br><br>CPS releases final guidelines with criteria to be used to determine various school actions.[F] | Applications for admission to schools for the 2013-14 academic year are due.[G] |
| **January 2013** | The Commission on School Utilization releases report with recommendations.[H]<br><br>CPS leads a new round of community engagement meetings in each school network.[I] | |
| **February 2013** | A pared down list of 129 elementary schools that could be closed is released. High schools and high-performing (Level 1) elementary schools are eliminated from the original list of 330 schools, based on recommendations from the Commission on School Utilization.[J] | |
| **March 2013** | A final list of schools is released with 51 elementary schools closings, two phasing out, and one closure of a high school program. Student Safety Transition Plans are released for each closing school, with information on the designated welcoming schools and investments to be made in each designated welcoming school.[K] | Illinois Standards Achievement Tests (ISAT) is administered.[L]<br><br>Notifications on whether students have been admitted to the schools to which they applied in December are mailed. |
| **April 2013** | A third phase of community meetings starts for each school on the closing list to gather feedback from parents and community members.[M]<br><br>State-mandated public hearings on each of the schools on the closing list start, presided by independent hearing officers. CPS staff present testimony followed by public comment.[N] | |
| **May 2013** | CPS updates transition plans for nine schools on the list, addressing specific issues uncovered during the public hearings.[O]<br><br>The Chicago Board of Education votes on the proposed schools to be closed. Forty-seven elementary schools and one high school program are chosen to be closed by the end of the academic year, and two more elementary schools will be phased out within two years. Four elementary schools are withdrawn from the list.[P]<br><br>Enrollment drives at closing and designated welcoming schools start right after the vote. Parents are also sent text messages, robo calls, phone banking calls, emails, letters, and mailers about enrollment in new schools.[Q] | |

| | About School Closings | Related Events |
|---|---|---|
| June 2013 | After June 12, families that have not yet enrolled in a school are automatically enrolled in the district designated welcoming schools, although parents can also register their children in other schools with available seats up until the beginning of the school year.[R] | |
| July 2013 | | A second application process is offered for magnet schools and magnet cluster schools that still have space available through the End-of-Year Citywide Options Program.[S] |
| August 2013 | | Start of the 2013-14 academic year |

A  Chicago Public Schools (2012, October 12).
B  Chicago Public Schools (2012, October 31).
C  Chicago Public Schools (2012, November 2).
D  Chicago Public Schools (2012, November 26).
E  Ahmed-Ullah (2012, December 5).
F  Chicago Public Schools (2012).
G  Chicago Public Schools (2012, December 11).
H  Chicago Public Schools (2013, January 10).
I  Chicago Public Schools (2013, January 11).
J  Chicago Public Schools (2013, February 13).
K  The transition plans can be found at http://www.cps.edu/qualityschools/Pages/Parents.aspx; Chicago Public Schools (2013, March 14); Chicago Public Schools (2013b, March 21); Chicago Public Schools (2013c, March 21); Lutton & Vevea (2013, March 21).
L  Illinois State Board of Education (2013).
M  Chicago Public Schools (2013, April 3).
N  Ahmed-Ullah (2013, April 15); Chicago Public Schools (2013, April 15); Chicago Public Schools (2013, April 29).
O  Chicago Public Schools (2013, May 20).
P  Chicago Public Schools (2013, May 22).
Q  Chicago Public Schools (2013, May 30).
R  An individual document was created for each school and made available to parents on the *Parents* page of the CPS website (http://www.cps.edu/qualityschools/Pages/Parents.aspx). The plan for John P. Altgeld Elementary School is used here as an example: http://schoolinfo.cps.edu/SchoolActions/Download.aspx?fid=2952 Chicago Public Schools (2013, July 12) and meeting with district staff on July 8, 2014.
S  Chicago Public Schools (2013, July 12).

## CPS Performance Policy

The *Performance, Remediation, and Probation Policy* was the district's school accountability policy in place at the time of school closures. The purpose was to measure school performance every year and to determine which schools were placed on probation.

Elementary schools were measured based on the following metrics: Performance levels on the Illinois Standards Achievement Tests (ISAT), performance trends on the ISAT, student academic growth on the ISAT, and attendance. Schools earned points for all these different metrics and an index was calculated based on the percentage of earned points. Schools were assigned one of three ratings: *"excellent standing"* or Level 1 if a school received at least 71 percent of available points, *"good standing"* or Level 2 if a school received between 50 and 70.9 percent, and *"probation"* or Level 3 if a school received less than 50 percent of available points.

Not all schools were rated. In order to receive a rating, an elementary school must have had data for enough metrics. The schools were evaluated on the percent of points earned using the metrics available to that school. Every year the rating was based on the prior year's data. For example, the 2012-13 performance policy rating used for decisions on school closures was based on 2011-12 data.

In the 2014-15 academic year, CPS introduced a new school accountability policy called School Quality Rating Policy (SQRP) for measuring annual school performance.

## Characteristics of Closed and Welcoming Schools

Of the 47 schools that closed, 36 were on probation and 11 had a *"good standing"* rating or Level 2 (**see Figure 1 and Table A.1 in Appendix A**). Among the 48 designated welcoming schools, 13 were on probation, 23 had a *"good standing"* rating, and 12 had the highest rating of *"excellent standing."* Of the closed schools, 22 were paired with a designated welcoming school of the same level, although the performance policy points were higher in most cases. The smallest difference in performance ratings between a closed school and an assigned welcoming school was between Mayo Elementary (the closed school) and Wells Preparatory Elementary School (the designated welcoming school). Both schools were on probation at the time the closings were announced and had the same performance policy points (26 points). The biggest difference in ratings can be seen between Bontemps Elementary School (the closed school) and Nicholson Elementary School (the designated welcoming school). Bontemps had a Level 3 rating with 17 points, while Nicholson had a Level 1 rating with 81 points. On average, the difference in performance policy points between a closed school and its associated welcoming school was 21 percentage points.

As stated above, the designated welcoming schools had to have enough available seats to accommodate the influx of displaced students. In fact, 41 of the 48 designated welcoming schools were labeled underutilized by district standards, with a utilization rate of less than 80 percent, while seven of the designated welcoming schools were regarded as efficient in terms of their utilization rate. Since some welcoming schools were also underutilized, 18 of them were on the February 2013 list of 129 elementary schools under consideration for closure.

Another important element was the distance between the designated welcoming school and the closed school. The welcoming school had to be within a mile of the closed school. In fact, in 14 cases the designated welcoming school relocated to the building of one of the closed schools because CPS determined these buildings were in better condition.[14] In some other instances, the designated welcoming school was not the closest school to students' residences or the closed school, even

---

14 In some instances, the district provided transportation for the students of the welcoming schools to attend their school at the new location.

**FIGURE 1**

**Most Designated Welcoming Schools had Higher Performance Policy Points Than Closed Schools, but the Differences Varied Substantially from No Difference to a Difference of 64 Points**

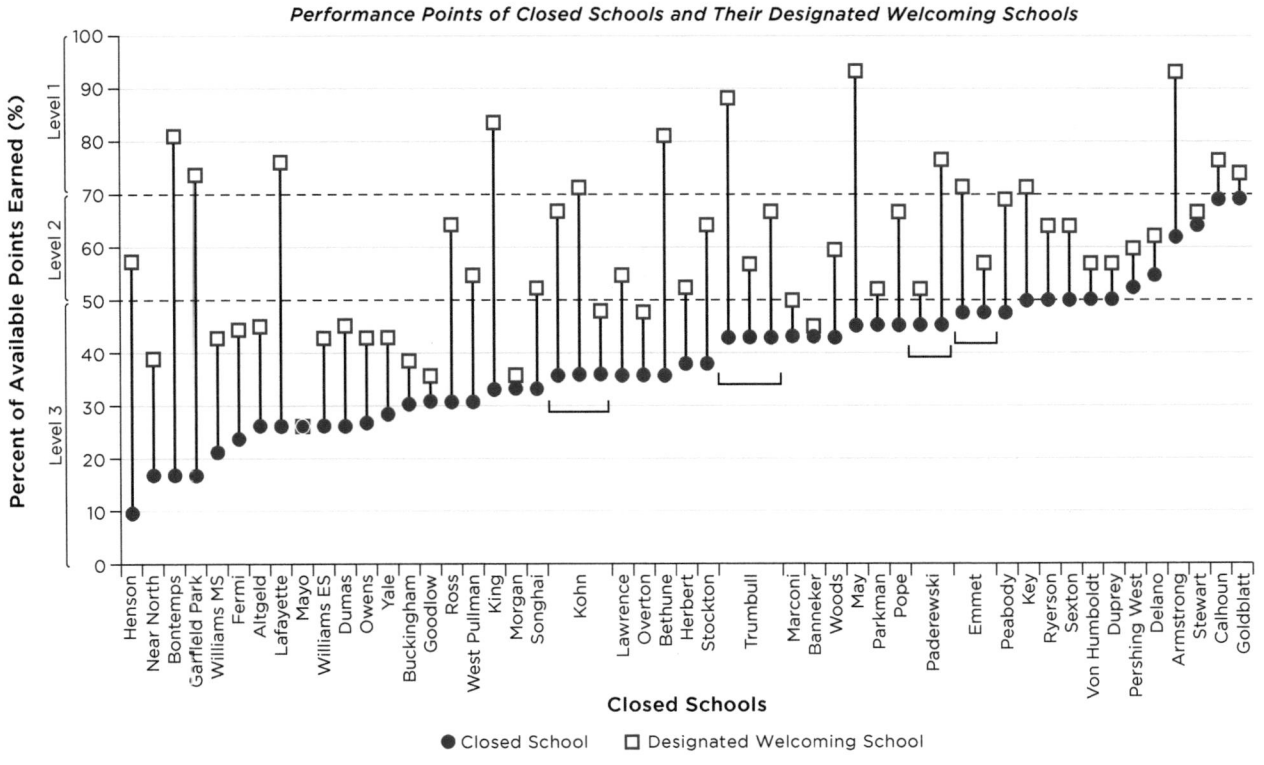

**Note:** The data used in this graph were based on the 2012-13 performance policy scores. Data were downloaded from the following CPS website: **http://cps.edu/-SchoolData/Pages/SchoolData.aspx**. In cases where a closed school had more than one designated welcoming school, the name of the closed school appears once with a bracket encompassing all of its welcoming schools. See Appendix A for characteristics of closed schools and designated welcoming schools.

though the designated welcoming school was within a mile of the closed school. For example, students from the closed school of Morgan Elementary were assigned to Ryder Elementary, which was the welcoming school. However, the geographic boundary that was previously associated with Morgan was reassigned to Gresham and Westcott elementary schools.[15] Some families lived closer to Gresham or Westcott than to Ryder. Therefore, the travel distance was further to reach the designated welcoming school than it would have been to reach other neighborhood schools.

When the designated welcoming school was beyond 0.8 miles from the closed school, the district offered transportation to the displaced students.[16] This happened at six of the closed schools (Bethune, Bontemps, King, Overton, Kohn, and Trumbull).[17] Transportation was only offered to current displaced students through their graduation from elementary school and not to kindergartners or new students who recently moved into a school's attendance area. It is important to note that the district's transportation plan was calculated based on the distance between the closed school and the designated welcoming school and was not based on the distance from students' residences. Buses picked up displaced students at a designated location—oftentimes their closed school and not their homes—to take them to the designated welcoming school locations.

---

15  This means that Ryder, Gresham, or Westcott, depending on the student's home address, were the new neighborhood schools for students living in the Morgan boundary; but only Ryder was the welcoming school.

16  In addition, transportation assistance continued to be offered to specific student populations (i.e., students with disabilities, students in temporary living situations, and NCLB-qualifying students) based on the CPS transportation policy.

17  Two other bus routes were added, based on safety concerns for students of Parkman and West Pullman. The transportation was provided for one year, with the possibility of an extension based on the safety environment after that time.

## Enrollment into Welcoming and Other CPS Schools

Immediately after the final vote to close schools was announced, CPS launched an enrollment campaign, sending text messages, robo calls, phone banking calls, emails, letters, mailers, and *"backpack drops"* with information about the end-of-year enrollment process. The district encouraged families to enroll their children into welcoming schools as soon as possible. As CPS CEO Barbara Byrd-Bennett stated in the press release: *"Early enrollment is key to a successful transition for students at their new Welcoming Schools this fall."* [18]

In letters sent to parents in March, immediately following the vote in May, and again in July, CPS outlined the plan for school closures and transitions.[19] For closed schools with more than one associated welcoming school, families were assigned to one specific welcoming school based on their home address and the new or existing geographic boundary areas drawn by the district. In the Summary of Action section of the transition plan, CPS wrote:

> Families are also encouraged to pursue other educational options at CPS that best meet their student's learning needs and family priorities. (Page 1 from the final CPS Transition Plan sent to parents on July 12, 2013)

Letters to parents also explained policies regarding parents' choice of schools. Because the final decision on closing schools came in May, many families missed the primary application deadline that took place in December for enrolling in new schools. However, CPS provided information about a secondary application process at the end of the school year in transition plans. This included information about dates of enrollment drives and the process for applying to the End-of-Year Citywide Options Program application process for magnet, magnet cluster, and open enrollment elementary schools that took place in July for those schools that had any open seats.

The transition plans sent to parents and guardians stated that, between May 22 and May 31, CPS would hold enrollment drives at each of the closed and welcoming schools. In addition, CPS would host enrollment fairs during the evenings to help parents select a school for their children. At the drives and fairs, parents were able to select their designated welcoming schools or other schools that had available open seats. There was also a web-based tool for families that showed the schools that were within a mile of the closed schools. Staff from the CPS network offices and the Office of Access and Enrollment were in attendance at these enrollment events to help parents enroll in new schools. After June 12, families that had not yet enrolled in a school were automatically enrolled in the district designated welcoming schools. Even still, they could try to enroll their children in other schools with open seats until the start of the school year on August 28. The transition plans and information packets also included materials about the End-of-Year Citywide Options Program summer application process. Students affected by school closures were told that they would have first priority.

In addition to the above information about school choices and enrollment, in the letters to families, CPS included more information about the designated welcoming schools, including safety and security measures, internal supports for students and schools, transportation options, and detailed academic and social/emotional learning plans for each of the welcoming schools.

## Investments in Designated Welcoming Schools

To provide safe travel to the welcoming schools for displaced students, CPS expanded the Safe Passage program that was already active in 35 high schools and four elementary school communities to include new routes near designated welcoming schools. CPS officials spent an additional $7.7 million to hire 600 more Safe Passage workers to stand along and patrol predetermined routes in areas where schools were closed.[20]

---

18 Chicago Public Schools (2013, May 30).
19 Transition plans ranged from six pages to 66 pages, depending on how many welcoming schools were assigned to the closed school.
20 Ahmed-Ullah (2013, August 9).

CPS hired community-based organizations and vendors to oversee the program. The job of Safe Passage workers was to make sure students were safe while they walked to and from school. According to the New Hope Community Service website, the Safe Passage program has two primary goals: (1) Reduce the likelihood that CPS students will become victims of violent incidents; and (2) create a safe, secure, and supportive school environment.[21] CPS mailed Safe Passage maps to every displaced student and posted the routes on their website.

In addition, the district invested in the welcoming schools with capital support, academic support, and other support to help specific student populations. Capital supports, such as upgraded technology, were introduced to help create a strong and supportive learning environment. Student-focused supports, such as tutoring, were intended to benefit students both inside and outside the classroom. Other supports, which were tailored to more specific student populations, were put in place to identify and address the unique needs of these students before the start of the school year. Seventeen designated welcoming schools received new International Baccalaureate (IB), Science, Technology, Engineering, and Math (STEM), and fine arts programs. The selection of welcoming schools and investments made in them were meant to attract families to these schools and to provide students with better educational opportunities. The next chapter discusses where students enrolled and whether or not those schools were the designated welcoming schools.

---

[21] New Hope Community Service Center Website (n.d.).

CHAPTER 2

# Enrollment Patterns After Schools Closed

With the final decision on which schools to close having occurred at the end of May, and with the end of the school year just a few weeks away, the district and families affected by the school closings started the process of enrolling in other schools for the 2013-14 academic year. The district wanted families to decide quickly where to enroll their children in order to ensure a smooth transition. Because close to 12,000 students were moving to a new school, many logistical issues had to be dealt with—such as moving furniture, hiring teachers, and making budgetary projections. By June 3, CPS announced that 78 percent of students were enrolled in a new school for the 2013-14 academic year.[22]

Among families that had enrolled by June 3, CPS reported that 83 percent of students enrolled their children in their designated welcoming school.[23] Recall that only the district designated welcoming schools received resources for Safe Passage and other improvements to accommodate students from closed schools. This chapter explores where families enrolled and how the new schools compared to the closed schools in terms of performance policy ratings or points. This chapter also begins to show some of the factors that explain these patterns, while the next chapter goes into a more in-depth presentation of what families said about enrolling students into new schools.

Using administrative data, this study follows all of the students who were enrolled in the 47 closed schools in grades K-7 at the end of the 2012-13 academic year.[24] These are the students who needed to reenroll into different elementary schools in fall 2013. (**See Appendix B** for a more detailed explanation of the sample of students included in the analyses. Also **see Appendix B** for the methods used and **the box entitled** *"Following Younger Students"* **on p.19**.) **Table 1** shows some of the characteristics of the displaced students and compares them to all K-7 students in CPS and to the K-7 students in the 129 underutilized Level 2 and 3 elementary schools that were originally targeted for potential closures in February.

**Students Affected by School Closures Were More Disadvantaged Than Typical CPS Students.** The data presented in Table 1 show that the students affected by closings were among the most disadvantaged students in CPS. However, other similar underutilized schools were also serving vulnerable students. Compared to the average CPS K-7 student, students affected by school closures were more likely to receive free or reduced-price lunch, to receive special education services, and to be old for their grade; they were less likely to have met the Illinois state standards on the ISAT math test. Their families were also more likely to have changed residences in the year prior to the school closings announcement, which suggests that they had less stability in housing. One-third of the closed schools housed a cluster program for students with the most serious disabilities.[25] In addition, the crime rate in the areas where the affected families lived was almost double the average for CPS students and a greater proportion of male adults were unemployed in these families' neighborhoods. The vast majority of students affected by school closures were African American.

---

22 Chicago Public Schools (2013, June 3).
23 Chicago Public Schools (2013, June 3).
24 The closed schools were serving students from pre-kindergarten (ages three and four) to grade eight. We focus on students in elementary grades (kindergarten and above) who needed to reenroll in a new elementary school. Because students in eighth grade moved to high school, they are not part of the study. Students ages three and four are not part of the sample because the district implemented a new enrollment process for the fall of 2013. See box entitled *"Following Younger Students"* on p. 19 for information.
25 Karp (2013, November 21).

**TABLE 1**

Characteristics of K-7 Students Enrolled in CPS in May 2013

|  | Students Enrolled in Closed Elementary Schools (10,708 students) | Students Enrolled in 129 Elementary Schools Initially Considered for Closure (33,564 students) | All K-7 CPS Students (235,067 students) |
|---|---|---|---|
| Percent African American | 88% | 88% | 39% |
| Percent Latino | 10% | 10% | 46% |
| Percent Receiving Special Education Services | 17% | 16% | 13% |
| Percent Receiving Free or Reduced-Price Lunch | 95% | 94% | 85% |
| Percent Old for Grade | 16% | 16% | 8% |
| ISAT Math (percent meeting/exceeding standards, Spring 2012) | 29% | 29% | 47% |
| Percent Changed Residences (May 2012–September 2012) | 14% | 12% | 7% |
| Crime Rate in Students' Neighborhoods (rate per 100 people) | 23 | 22 | 13 |
| Percent Males in Students' Neighborhoods Who Are Employed | 60% | 60% | 75% |

**Note:** Based on CPS administrative data, census data, and police crime data. See Appendix B for a description of the variables.

Students from all of the schools that were initially targeted for closure shared similar characteristics. The schools that were underutilized and not in *"excellent standing"* served a larger share of vulnerable students than other schools in CPS. As we mentioned, part of the controversy surrounding the school closures was the decision to close schools in some of the most struggling areas in the city. This evidence confirms that the neighborhoods most affected by closings show high levels of crime and poverty. Consequently, this closings policy affected some of the most vulnerable students in the district.

**There was no increase in the number of families that decided to leave CPS after schools closed.** A number of students left the district after schools closed, but the rate of transfers out of the district was similar to prior years at the closed schools. Of the students enrolled in grades K-7, 94 percent reenrolled in a CPS school by September 2013 (**see Figure 2**). Even though this percentage is lower than what other CPS elementary schools experienced the same year (96 percent), it is comparable to previous years when, on average, 94 percent of the student population attending those schools in May continued their education in the district.[26]

**In the fall of 2013, more students attended a Level 3 (probation) school than were originally assigned to them.** In the 2012-13 academic year, when attending a closed school, 78 percent of students attended a Level 3 school, 22 percent of students attended a Level 2 school, and none of the students attended a Level 1 school (**see Figure 3**). These 10,062 students who reenrolled in CPS were assigned to higher-rated welcoming schools. If all students had enrolled into their designated welcoming schools in the fall of 2013, 30 percent would have attended a Level 3 school, 43 percent would have attended

---

[26] See Appendix B, Table B.2, for a description of the statistical analyses carried out to determine whether there was an increase in the number of families leaving CPS after schools closed.

FIGURE 2

After Schools Closed, 94 Percent of Students Reenrolled in CPS Schools—A Percentage That Is Comparable to Previous Years

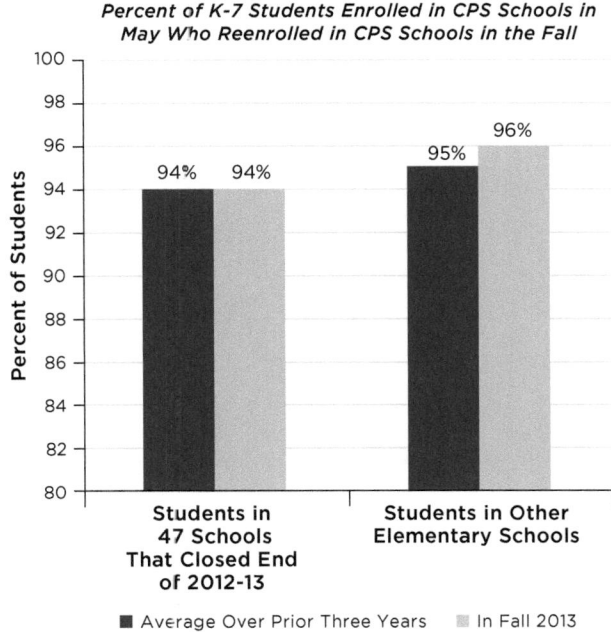

*Percent of K-7 Students Enrolled in CPS Schools in May Who Reenrolled in CPS Schools in the Fall*

■ Average Over Prior Three Years   ■ In Fall 2013

**Note:** Data come from CPS administrative records. We followed students who were enrolled in CPS schools in grades K-7 in May and checked how many reenrolled in any CPS school in the fall of the following academic year. Bars on the left represent students who attended the 47 closed schools, while the bars on the right represent students who attended other CPS elementary schools. The dark bars show the average reenrollment rates in the prior three years, while the light bars show the reenrollment rates in the fall of 2013, after school closures took place. Appendix B shows the statistical analysis carried out to test the hypothesis of whether fewer students reenrolled in CPS after schools closed.

FIGURE 3

In the Fall of 2013, More Students Attended a Level 3 School Than Originally Assigned Through the Designated Welcoming Schools

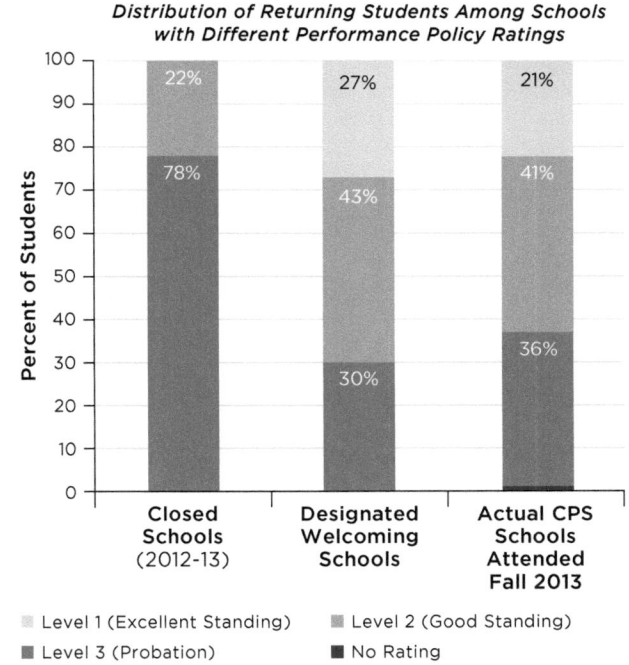

*Distribution of Returning Students Among Schools with Different Performance Policy Ratings*

■ Level 1 (Excellent Standing)   ■ Level 2 (Good Standing)
■ Level 3 (Probation)   ■ No Rating

**Note:** Calculations using CPS administrative data based on 10,062 students who enrolled in a CPS school in fall 2013. Performance levels are those schools received in the 2012-13 academic year, based on school data from the 2011-12 academic year.

a Level 2 school, and 27 percent would have attended a Level 1 school. However, the schools that many students actually attended were rated lower than the schools to which they were assigned. In reality, more students (36 percent vs. 30 percent) enrolled in a Level 3 school than the district intended. A few students attended schools that did not have a performance policy rating; these were relatively new schools without enough data to get a rating.

Recall that prior research has found that students who relocated from closed schools to substantially higher-performing schools showed improvements in their academic performance. However, when students attended schools of similar performance levels as their closed schools, they did not show improved performance. In some cases, these students experienced adverse effects on their test scores after schools closed.[27] When Chicago closed schools in the summer of 2013, 21 percent of students from the closed schools attended a top-rated school (Level 1). However, it is a lower percentage than what the district initially planned.

A more nuanced picture of the differences between the performance of the district designated welcoming schools and other schools students enrolled in emerges by examining the differences in performance policy points. **Table 2** shows the differences in performance policy points between closed schools, designated welcoming schools, and the schools students actually

---

**27** de la Torre & Gwynne (2009); Kirshner et al. (2010); Barrow et al. (2011); Engberg et al. (2012); Brummet (2014).

**TABLE 2**

Most Students Attended Schools With Higher Performance Policy Points Than the Closed School, but Lower Performance Policy Points Than the Designated School

|  | Performance Policy Points Difference Between Designated School and Closed School | Performance Policy Points Difference Between Attended School and Designated School | Performance Policy Points Difference Between Attended School and Closed School |
|---|---|---|---|
| **Average Point Difference** | 21 | -3 | 18 |
| **Students Designated/Attended a Much Higher-Rated School** (difference >= 20 performance policy points) | 39% | 4% | 36% |
| **Students Designated/Attended a Lower-Rated School** | 0% | 23% | 7% |
| **Number of Students** | 10,062 | 9,896 | 9,896 |

**Note:** Calculations using CPS administrative data. Performance levels are those schools received in the 2012-13 academic year, based on school data from the 2011-12 academic year. There are fewer students represented in the last two columns because some students enrolled in a CPS school with no performance policy rating.

attended. On average, students were assigned to schools with a performance policy rating that was 21 points higher, with all students assigned to higher-rated or equally-rated schools. Moreover, 39 percent of students were assigned to schools that were at least 20 points higher than the closed school.

Nearly all displaced students (93 percent) attended schools with higher performance policy points than the closed schools, with 7 percent of students attending a school with lower points than their school that closed. However, only about one-third of displaced students attended schools with at least 20 performance points higher than the closed school.

Students who enrolled in other CPS schools were more likely to attend lower-rated schools. A small group of students (4 percent) enrolled in schools with at least 20 performance points higher than the designated welcoming school. But a sizable group of students (one-quarter) attended schools that had fewer performance policy points than their designated welcoming school.

## Enrollment into Designated Welcoming Schools

Of the 10,062 students who reenrolled in CPS in the fall of 2013, 66 percent enrolled into their designated welcoming school. This rate of enrollment into designated welcoming schools varied greatly from one closed school to another, ranging from 6 percent to 90 percent.

One-quarter of displaced students enrolled in a neighborhood elementary school other than their designated welcoming school, 4 percent found seats in charter schools, and 4 percent enrolled in magnet schools. Besides the 48 designated welcoming schools, the K-7 students from closed schools enrolled in 311 other CPS elementary schools across the city.

Among the strongest factors that explained the variation in the enrollment rates in designated welcoming schools was whether the designated welcoming school moved into the building of the closed school so that the commute to school was not affected for these families. Of students in this situation, 83 percent attended their designated school. In contrast, only half of the students who had to travel to a new building for their welcoming school enrolled in that school. Similarly, the closer the designated welcoming school was to a student's residence, the more likely that student would enroll in the designated school. Seventy-six percent of students enrolled in their designated school when the designated school was 0.5 miles or less from students' residences, vs. 53 percent when the distance was longer than 0.5 miles (**see Figure 4**).

Families were more likely to enroll into designated schools where reported safety levels were higher than the district average, compared to designated schools with average or below-average safety levels.[28] Among students assigned to a designated welcoming school

## Following Younger Students

There were 1,753 students enrolled in pre-K in the 47 schools that closed in 2013. We have not included these three- and four-year-old students in the main analyses because their enrollment process changed that year and because they do not tend to follow the same patterns as older elementary school students—meaning that they enrolled in lower numbers in the same school the following year.

An analysis of their enrollment patterns indicates that these families were less likely to reenroll in a school in the district (83 vs. 94 percent for students in grades K-7). However, this reenrollment rate for pre-K students was similar to the average rate for three- and four-year-old students in these schools in prior years.

Of the families that reenrolled their children in a CPS school, 61 percent did so in the designated welcoming school. This number is lower than the 66 percent observed for students in elementary grades. The percent of students enrolling in their designated welcoming school is much lower for four-year-old students, who were moving from a pre-K program to a kindergarten program as part of a regular elementary school. This reenrollment rate for four-year old students was 52 percent.

|  | All 3- and 4-Year-Olds (1,753 students) | 3-Year-Olds (799 students) | 4-Year-Olds (954 students) |
| --- | --- | --- | --- |
| **Percent Reenrolling in CPS Schools** | | | |
| - Fall of 2013 After Schools Closed | 83% | 75% | 90% |
| - Prior Three Years in the Same Schools | 85% | 81% | 89% |
| **Percent Enrolling in Designated Welcoming Schools** (among those who reenrolled in CPS) | 61% | 73% | 52% |

with an above-average safety level, 79 percent of students enrolled in the designated school compared to 56 percent who were assigned to schools with average or below-average levels of safety.

Families that were more mobile and those with a residence outside the attendance area of the closed school were less likely to enroll in the designated welcoming schools. These families were more likely to be further away from the designated welcoming schools than others; but, even after distance is taken into account, they were still less likely to enroll. The next chapter will describe in more detail some barriers families faced when enrolling into designated welcoming schools associated with mobility and attendance areas.

Not many of the other designated welcoming school characteristics we examined made a difference in explaining whether families enrolled into these schools or not. Among them, we examined whether having a STEM or International Baccalaureate (IB) program attracted more families to these schools and whether being on the previous school closing list made families less likely to enroll in these schools. None of these characteristics were related in a statistically significant way to the likelihood that a student enrolled in the designated welcoming school (**see Appendix B**).

Two designated welcoming school characteristics were significantly related to enrolling in the designated welcoming school: the difference in performance policy points between the closed school and the designated school and whether transportation was offered. It was somewhat surprising that students were less likely to attend schools that offered transportation from the closed school. Recall that the district offered transportation when designated schools were 0.8 miles from the closed school, as well as for a couple of closed schools less than 0.8 miles away from their designated welcoming school, owing to safety concerns. This transportation was usually offered from the closed school, not the

---

**28** These reports on safety come from student responses to My Voice, My School surveys. See Appendix B for an explanation of this variable.

**FIGURE 4**

Convenience and Distance Were Top Factors Contributing to Whether Students Enrolled in Designated Welcoming Schools or Not

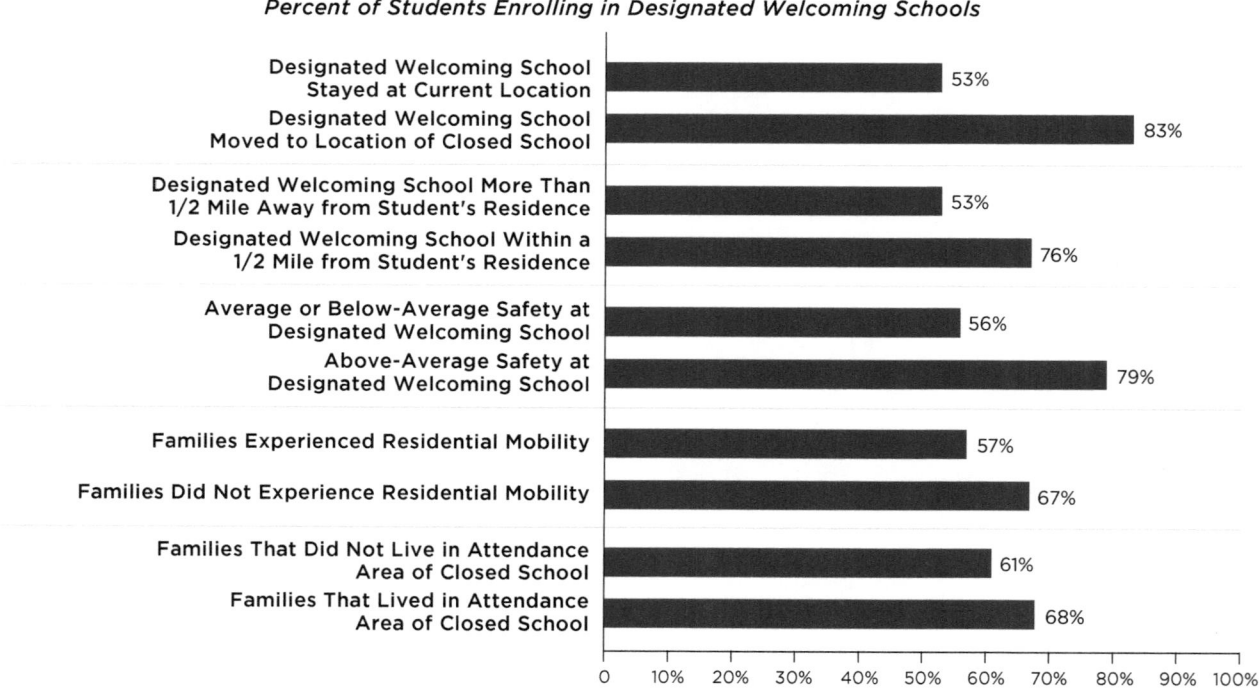

**Note:** Calculations using CPS administrative data and survey data. Appendix B shows the statistical analysis predicting whether families enrolled in designated welcoming schools or not. Variables shown here are the ones that were statistically significant in the model.

students' residences. Perhaps the offer of transportation could not offset the problems of sending children to distant, unfamiliar neighborhoods. As will be described in Chapter 3, proximity to school and familiarity with the neighborhood were common factors that families considered when deciding on new schools for their children.

It was also surprising that students assigned to higher-rated schools were less likely to attend those schools; the larger the difference in performance policy points between the closed school and the designated one, the more likely students were to attend schools other than their designated welcoming school. This may seem counterintuitive. If these ratings are good indicators of school performance, one should expect that families would be more likely to enroll in the highest-rated schools. But as discussed in Chapter 3, families judge school quality on more than performance points. In addition, some families really wanted their children to attend these schools but encountered some barriers to enrolling into them. Chapter 3 describes what factors families considered and weighed when deciding where to send their children to a new school, as well as what barriers and constraints they faced in the process.

In addition, families that lived in neighborhoods with more schools in the vicinity (especially Level 1 and 2 schools) were less likely to enroll in the designated welcoming school. We do not know whether these schools had available seats; this reflects only that there were other schools near their residences. However, it does suggest that these families had more options within their neighborhood.

It is worth noting that no student characteristics helped explain why students enrolled into designated welcoming schools or chose other schools. Whether students had above or below average test scores, whether they were receiving special education services, or whether they were receiving free or reduced-price lunch were not significantly related to their likelihood of attending the designated welcoming schools. Enrollment patterns rested more on school characteristics than on student characteristics.

## Enrollment into CPS Schools That Were Not Designated Welcoming Schools

This section examines the 3,464 students who enrolled in CPS schools that were not designated welcoming schools and explores the factors associated with enrollment in higher- or lower-rated schools. These students enrolled in 311 schools across the city, 20 percent in Level 1 schools—the highest rated schools—35 percent in Level 2 schools, 39 percent in Level 3 schools, and 6 percent in schools with no available rating (**see Figure 5**). As we saw in the previous section, these students were more likely to have been assigned to higher-rated schools than the students who actually enrolled in the designated welcoming schools. Most enrolled in schools with lower performance policy points than their designated welcoming school. These students were particularly likely to attend a Level 3 school.

Even though students who attended other CPS schools enrolled in lower-rated schools than the designated one, the school they attended was more likely to be higher-rated than their closed school (**see Table 3**).

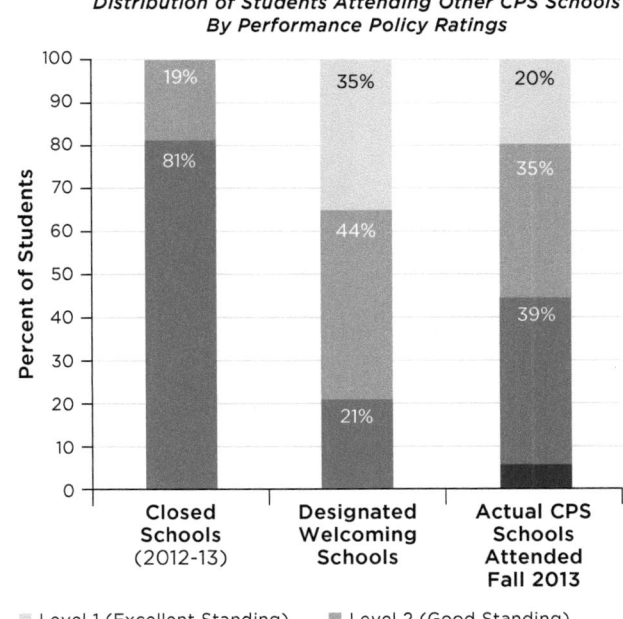

**FIGURE 5**

**Most Students Who Did Not Attend Their Designated Welcoming School Enrolled in Lower-Rated Schools**

*Distribution of Students Attending Other CPS Schools By Performance Policy Ratings*

**Note:** Calculations used CPS administrative data for the 3,464 students who enrolled in other CPS schools. Performance levels are those schools received in the 2012-13 academic year, based on school data from the 2011-12 academic year.

**TABLE 3**

**More Than a Fifth of Students Who Did Not Enroll in Their Designated School Attended Schools That Had Lower Performance Policy Points Than the Closed Schools**

| | Performance Policy Points Difference Between Designated School and Closed School | Performance Policy Points Difference Between Attended School and Designated School | Performance Policy Points Difference Between Attended School and Closed School |
|---|---|---|---|
| Average Difference | 25 | -9 | 16 |
| Students Designated/Attended a Much Higher-Rated School (difference >= 20 performance policy points) | 49% | 9% | 40% |
| Students Designated/Attended a Lower-Rated School | 0% | 64% | 22% |
| Number of Students | 3,464 | 3,298 | 3,298 |

**Note:** Calculations using CPS administrative data for the 3,464 students who enrolled in other CPS schools. Performance levels are those schools received in the 2012-13 academic year, based on school data from the 2011-12 academic year. There are fewer students represented in the last two columns because some students enrolled in a CPS school with no performance policy rating.

On average, students attended a school 9 performance points lower than their designated one, but 16 performance points higher than their closed school. However, as we described in the earlier section, a group of students (22 percent of students among those in non-designated schools) attended lower-rated schools than the closed school.

Students who lived in neighborhoods with few high- rated schools were more likely to attend non-designated welcoming schools with a Level 3 rating. One factor that explains the fact that families ended up in lower-rated schools has to do with the number of school options in the neighborhood (see Appendix B for the statistical analyses). Figure 6 shows the enrollment in different schools by the availability of different school options within half a mile. Those families with no Level 1 school within half a mile of their home were more likely to enroll in a Level 3 school (45 percent of students did); only 10 percent of these students enrolled in a Level 1 school. In contrast, of those families with at least one Level 1 school within half a mile, one-third enrolled in a Level 1 school while one-third enrolled in a Level 3 school.

A school's location played a role in families' decisions about whether to enroll their children into designated welcoming schools or into other CPS schools. It was important for families to attend a school that was in close proximity to their residence (see Chapter 3). This was true for many families—whether they attended the designated welcoming school, whether they attended another CPS school that was higher-rated than the designated one, or whether they attended another CPS school that was lower-rated than the designated one. Looking at the distances from families' residences to schools attended (if not at the designated one), there was virtually no difference regardless of whether

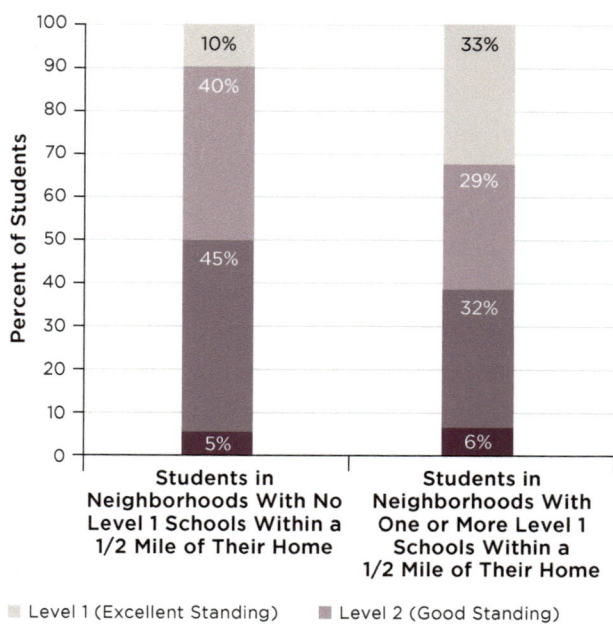

FIGURE 6

Students Who Lived in Neighborhoods With Fewer High-Rated Schools Were More Likely to Attend Other CPS Schools With a Level 2 or 3 Rating

*Distribution of Students Attending Other CPS Schools by Performance Policy Ratings and by Whether Neighborhood Had High-Rated Options*

**Note:** Calculations used CPS administrative data. Appendix B shows the statistical analysis behind whether families that did not enroll in designated welcoming schools attended schools with different levels of performance.

students attended a higher- or lower-rated school. Half of the students who attended a school that was higher-rated than their designated school were 0.51 miles from the school attended in the fall; half of the students who attended a lower-rated school than the closed one were 0.54 miles from the school attended in the fall.

The next chapter describes the reasons families' offered for enrolling in new schools and what barriers, if any, they faced. In particular, we will learn more about how distance, safety, and transportation factored into families, thinking about selecting a new school for their children.

CHAPTER 3

# Understanding Enrollment Patterns after Schools Closed

In theory, the school closings policy offered families a choice to send their children to the district designated welcoming school or to other schools with open seats. The process, however, was more akin to an orchestrated choice—by assigning students to higher-rated schools within a mile of their closed school, CPS anticipated that families would choose to enroll in these welcoming schools. To make them more appealing to families, CPS also invested resources in these welcoming schools for new programs, air conditioning, and technology in addition to providing Safe Passage routes. Although the majority of students did enroll into their designated welcoming school, we learned in Chapter 2 that 34 percent of displaced families enrolled their children into other schools in the district.

Why did students end up either in designated welcoming schools or in other schools in the district? We know from other research on school choice, more generally, that families factor in school quality, but also consider a variety of other criteria prior to making their final school decisions. These criteria range from the distance between homes and schools, to peer group preferences, racial composition of schools, and availability of transportation. **See box, "What Families Considered When Selecting a New School for Their Children," on p.25** for a visual highlighting what factors the families we interviewed considered.[29] Some displaced families may have also faced barriers or constraints that prevented them from enrolling in certain schools. In this chapter, we describe the reasons families either enrolled their children into a designated welcoming school or opted for other CPS schools. What criteria mattered to families when thinking about new schools for their children? What barriers did families face when trying to enroll their children into desired schools?

To answer these questions, we interviewed 95 families affected by the school closings and asked them about the information they received, the barriers and limitations they faced, and their decision-making process around enrolling their children into a new school. The 95 families we spoke with were from 12 closed schools (six to eight families per school). More details about the families we interviewed are provided in **Table C.1**, along with a more thorough description of our qualitative sample and analysis in **Appendix C**.

## Why Did Families Enroll Their Children into Designated Welcoming Schools?

According to the families we interviewed, children were enrolled into a designated welcoming school for one of three reasons: (1) Parents/guardians actively chose to enroll their children into the welcoming school because it matched the criteria they were looking for in schools; (2) parents/guardians believed they did not have a choice to enroll their children elsewhere; or (3) parents/guardians faced constraints or barriers that limited their options for other schools.

**Many families chose to enroll their children into their designated welcoming school because the school matched the criteria they were looking for in schools.** When asked why they ultimately enrolled their children into the designated welcoming schools, many interviewees said that their designated welcoming schools fit their children's needs and family priorities. These priorities included being close to home, having personal connections to the school, and academics.

**Close to Home.** Most of the families that chose to send their children to their designated welcoming school did so because the school was close to their home.

---

[29] Hastings, Kane, & Staiger (2005); Rothstein (2004); Sikkink & Emerson (2008); Tedin & Weiher (2004).

Having a school close to home was more than a matter of convenience; many families considered it to be a necessity. For example, one family member described why she chose the school closest to her mother's home:

> I wanted to have a support system in place. If I need my mom to pick my daughter up, [the designated welcoming school] would be closer to my mom's. If for any reason I couldn't pick her up, I wanted to have a support system in place. If I get stuck in snow coming from school, you know, my mom could take a cab, pick her up, and zip back because it's just that close. And that's the reason I chose that [school]...

Being close to home was not only about convenience but also about families' realities. Parents and guardians worried about being able to get children to and from school when the weather was bad or when their children got sick.

**Personal Connections to the School.** The second most common reason families chose to enroll their children into designated welcoming schools was because of personal connections to the school. For instance, families talked about staff and students from the closed schools transferring to the designated welcoming schools (**see Vignette, *"Familiar Faces Make New School Feel More Welcoming"* on p.27**). One mother wanted her child to see a familiar face so that the school did not feel like a completely new environment. Besides having the connection with others in the school and the continuity of having some of the same staff in the welcoming schools, overwhelmingly parents talked about feeling more comfortable sending their children to a school where they already knew other adults and students. For example, one mother said:

> They [the designated welcoming school] allowed most of the staff [from the closed school] to come there, and allowed them to work there as part of their staff. It was a lot of [closed school] staff that I knew, that I felt comfortable with my child being around people that he knew...

Having the continuity of care and familiarity with the closed school staff in the new environment was particularly important for families with special needs children. Several interviewees said that they picked the designated welcoming school primarily because the closed school's special education teachers would be at the new school. These families worried less about getting the necessary supports and services in the new school if they had the same teachers or support personnel than they would have with unfamiliar staff. Having that personal connection put their minds at ease.

In a similar vein, some families chose their designated welcoming school because they had family connections to the school. For example, some interviewees had family members who worked at the welcoming schools or had nieces and nephews or other family members that attended the schools. As one interviewee stated, *"I didn't want to send my daughter anywhere else where she didn't know anybody, period."*

**Academics.** Some families picked their designated welcoming school because they had higher test scores than other options in their neighborhood or had specific academic programs that suited their children's interests and needs. For example, one family member stated that she would not send her child to another Level 3 school. Instead, she said, *"I just wanted to make sure that when it came to her eighth-grade year she was able to achieve the scores and do whatever it is that she needed to do."* Similarly, another interviewee talked about choosing the welcoming school because it had higher test scores than many other options in the area. She also heard good things about the school academically from her social network. She ultimately chose the welcoming school for her daughter, she said, because, *"I think they had more to offer her—their grading, scores, more structure—so that she would get more of what she needs."* Some families decided to enroll their children into the designated welcoming school because they liked specific classes or particular academic programs, such as STEM or IB. Other families chose the welcoming school based on after-school programs or enrichment activities.

Besides having higher test scores and specific academic offerings, several interviewees said they chose the designated welcoming school because they thought their children would receive more individualized or one-on-one

## What Families Considered When Selecting a New School for Their Children

The following image is a word cloud that captures all of the criteria or factors that families said mattered to them when considering schools for their children. The font sizes are related to how many times families mentioned a particular criterion or factor, with the largest fonts representing the most talked about factor. For example, a safe commute was mentioned by the majority of families while diversity of the school community was less frequently raised.

Overall, finding a school close to home was the most important consideration for families. In addition, safety was vital, along with connections to people at the new schools and individualized academic support for children. As families talked about what mattered to them as they considered schools for their children, four primary categories emerged:

1. Practical considerations, such as finding a school close to home with a safe commute and/or affordable transportation options;

2. Personal connections with the new school, including friends and staff from closed schools who transferred to the new schools;

3. Academic considerations, like special programs/services or supports, individual instruction or academic attention from teachers, high tests scores, or other official academic performance measures; and

4. School culture indicators, such as discipline policies, good communication practices between staff and families, and welcoming school environments.

*[Word cloud with terms including: FamilyConnections, ClosedSchoolStudentsTranferred, School, PerformanceMeasures, ClosedSchoolStaffTransferred, BullyingFighting, TransportationCosts, ClassesCurriculum, WelcomingEnvironment, Diversity, SiblingsTogether, NoTransfers, GoodTeachers, CloseToHome, GoodCommunication, ClassSizes, DisciplinePractices, AfterSchoolPrograms, Ratings, SafeCommute, IndividualizedAcademicAttention, SpecialEducationSupports]*

academic attention from teachers in these schools. Many families wanted to make sure their children received the support and attention they needed to learn and improve their grades and test scores. Families used the terms *"catered to children," "top performing," "good school,"* and *"caring teachers"* to describe the academic environment at their designated welcoming school.

### Some families believed they did not have a choice.

Although many families enrolled their children into the designated welcoming school because the school fit with their priorities and needs, some families did so because they believed they did not have a choice. These family members indicated that the reason their children enrolled at one of the district designated welcoming schools was because they *"had to"* attend the school the district picked for them. When parents read the letters or heard information about the district assigning welcoming schools to families, many believed that meant other options were off the table. As one mother explained:

**Chapter 3** | Understanding Enrollment Patterns after Schools Closed

> We were basically just told all the kids that went to [closed school], they all have to go to [the district designated welcoming school] now. And I was not happy about that. My children were not happy about it. I basically thought I wasn't given a list of options at all, other than that school. And I'm not satisfied with that school. So I kind of feel like I was forced to put my kids over there, like the decision was made for me, basically. And that was the only decision I had.

This mother said she would have considered other options had she known that they were available to her. Another mother expressed a similar sentiment, saying that she did get the letter about the welcoming school and knew that her children would be automatically enrolled at the welcoming school. When asked if she had considered other schools for her children, she stated, *"No, they told us that we needed to go to that school. We may have wanted to go to a different school, but they gave us that one."* She went on to say that her daughters' names were already at the district designated welcoming school; so, therefore, she did not believe that she had an option to send them elsewhere.

**Other families faced constraints or barriers that limited their school options and made them feel like they had no choice.** Families that believed that the district designated welcoming school was *"chosen"* for them did not take the time to consider other schools because they thought they had no other options. Other families, however, talked about having no agency or choice in the process because they were limited by the lack of options in their community or faced constraints or barriers getting into other desired schools.

**Safety Concerns.** Some family members said that the welcoming school was the only decent option in their area because of safety concerns. In some neighborhoods, drug trafficking and gang issues are major concerns. For these families, the welcoming school may have been seen as the only safe choice because it was closest to their homes and/or the district provided Safe Passage routes for families enrolled at welcoming schools. For instance, when asked why she did not consider other schools in her area, one mother said:

> Neither one of those schools are in good areas, I mean I don't know too much about the school, but I know it's a lot of fighting and a lot of gang-related stuff, and I just didn't even want to be bothered with that, so [the welcoming school] was still close to my house, in walking distance.

Safety for many parents/guardians was not just about crime statistics and gang activity. Family preferences for proximity to home and safety stem not only from spatial aspects of geography (i.e., commute times) but also from the deep connections families have to their neighborhoods and communities.[30] For instance, when asked about any concerns she had sending her son to schools she was considering, one mother said, *"...my seventh-grader is almost six feet tall, and I don't want anybody confusing him [for a gang member]."* Because of her social network and neighborhood connections, she felt safer sending her son to the designated welcoming school that was close to home where everyone knew who he was and knew that he was not a troublemaker. At the same time, she felt she had no other real options because of where she lived.

**Lack of Transportation.** Many families said that their options were limited primarily because the district did not provide transportation to other schools. One mother explained that she was worried about sending her children to the district designated welcoming school in terms of safety; but, because she did not have a car or a job, she could not afford to get her children to a different school. Another father expressed a similar sentiment saying, *"I really didn't get any choices. I didn't get any choices because we already lived so far."* Not being able to afford transportation costs limited many families to schools directly in or very near their neighborhoods. As one mother explained:

---

**30** Bell (2007).

MRS. BAKER: A VIGNETTE

# Familiar Faces Make New School Feel More Welcoming

Mrs. Baker (a pseudonym) has three children, two of whom were directly affected by the school closings. The children were in grades three and seven when they found out that their school was on the potential closings list. Mrs. Baker was saddened when she heard the news because the teachers and staff were like a *"family"* to her children. Everyone—from the security guard to the teachers and the principal to the secretary—knew her children's names.

She liked that the teachers were on top of her kids if they were struggling academically, would call her when they were concerned, and would get them tutoring or pull out services when necessary. When her children heard that their school was on the potential closing list, they participated actively in protests and meetings to try to keep the school open. Once the final list of schools was announced and their school was on it, the staff turned toward keeping parents informed about their options and stayed on top of making sure every child had signed up for the new school they would attend the following fall.

Because her children had a very hard time dealing with their neighborhood school closing, Mrs. Baker was very intent on finding the right school for her children. Her main concern with the school was safety. She said, *"I do know it's a little bit of a bad neighborhood, there are a lot of gang bangers that stand on the corner...So that was my main concern."*

At first, Mrs. Baker considered putting her children into a Catholic school close to her home because the class sizes were small and she believed that students would get more one-on-one attention from teachers. Financially, however, she and her family could not afford it. After ruling out the private school, Mrs. Baker called the designated welcoming school to ask some questions about the transition process and Safe Passage routes. When the phone was answered, she was very pleased to hear a familiar voice on the other end of the line. She explained:

> When I called, the secretary from [the closed school] is the one that answered the phone, and I said, 'oh my God, you're there, do you work there?' She's like 'yeah, security came here, a lot of teachers came this way.' And I was like, 'you know what, I'm not even going to ask any more questions, like my kids are going there!' I felt so much better knowing that a lot of the staff from [the closed school] went to [the designated welcoming school].

The secretary was able to give her all of the details about the new school and talked her through how the Safe Passage routes worked, so Mrs. Baker felt much more at ease. In the end, Mrs. Baker chose to send her children to the designated welcoming school because she felt that having the connection and continuity with the closed school staff would be beneficial for her children: *"When I heard her voice and then she told me everybody else was there, I was like, you know what... when do they start? They'll be there."*

> Everything else [my children] would have to take public transportation, and then you know, it's kind of hard getting six children around on a CTA bus, you know? And paying bus fare and everything without being able to provide a school bus for the children.

**Supports and/or Services for Children with IEPs.** Families that have children with IEPs talked about having limited options and a harder time finding schools with the adequate supports and services needed for their children. One interviewee said her son was assigned to the designated welcoming school, but she worried that the school would not have what he needed. Other families with special needs children had to rule other schools out because they did not have the services and supports:

> I actually had a list of the schools, but when I counted out the schools that I tried for him to go to, they didn't have programs for special needs…later I see like five schools in the area that I know have these programs, so to speak, but it's too far. It's too far.

**Attendance Area Boundaries.** In addition to transportation costs and limited options for families with special needs children, interviewees also talked about enrolling into their district designated welcoming schools by default, not by choice, simply because it was the only school in their neighborhood that they could get into. This parent put it succinctly, saying:

> Because CPS always had some type of boundary area around these schools and the school that they select for you isn't always the greatest school, it's what's left…there wasn't anything else really to choose from, you know, if you wanted your kids really to have an education.

This parent said he was turned away at other schools in the community because they were outside of his attendance area and did not have enough available seats.

In addition to the above, in cases where closed schools had more than one designated welcoming school, some displaced families from these closed schools were confused when they were assigned to one of the designated welcoming schools and were not able to choose among the list of other welcoming schools. For example, one interviewee said that her closed school had three different designated welcoming schools. She believed that she had *"three choices"* but, when she approached one of the welcoming schools, she was told that the school was not her designated welcoming school and was outside of her attendance area—even though it was closer to her home than the welcoming school the district assigned to her. Many of these families thought that they should have been able to choose from among the welcoming schools rather than the district assigning one to each family **(see Table A.1 in Appendix A** showing which closed schools had more than one designated welcoming school and also which designated welcoming schools were located outside of some families' attendance area boundaries). In some cases, families were allowed to enroll into a welcoming school that was neither their designated welcoming school nor in their attendance area; in other cases, families were told that they had to enroll their children into a specific designated school. This inconsistency was confusing to many families.

**Limited Time to Pick New Schools.** Many families said that their options were limited based on a lack of time to look for other schools because the final announcement of closed schools came late in the school year. In addition, because the timeframe to look for other options was truncated, families faced barriers getting into other schools because the lottery application for some schools had passed and because of limited open seats at other schools in their area. One family member said she felt she did not have time to actively seek other school options for her children, explaining, *"I think I would have taken them out [of the welcoming school] if I could have gotten them to another options school, but I just, it was just over, there were no options for me."* Another interviewee also talked about the lack of time to look for other schools, saying, *"It's kind of too late to put them anywhere else."*

Overall, we heard two divergent messages from families that enrolled into welcoming schools—families either actively chose their designated welcoming school or they felt they had no choice, either because they were misinformed about having options or because they faced barriers or constraints getting into other schools they were considering. For some families, the school that CPS designated for them happened to have what that family wanted in a school; whereas, for other families, the welcoming school did not necessarily fit, but there were no other options.

## Why Did Families Enroll Their Children In Other CPS Schools?

By assigning welcoming schools to each closed school, the district encouraged families to enroll in these schools that had higher performance policy ratings and where investments were made. But why did some families enroll their children into other CPS schools? Similar to families that attended welcoming schools, some parents arrived at other CPS schools because they faced constraints or barriers getting into their designated welcoming schools while others chose to enroll their children into other CPS schools.

**Some families enrolled into other CPS schools because they faced constraints or barriers getting into their designated welcoming schools.** Among our interviewees, approximately half of the families that enrolled their children into schools that were higher-rated than their welcoming schools and about a third of families that enrolled into schools that were lower-rated than their welcoming schools did so because they faced constraints or barriers getting into their welcoming schools. The major barrier these families faced was that they moved out of the attendance area of the closed school or they did not live in the attendance area of the closed school in the first place. Other families that lived outside of the attendance area of the closed school could get into their welcoming schools, but either they could not afford transportation costs to get to the school or they felt that the commute to school was too far and unsafe for their children because the welcoming school was even further away from their residence than the closed school.

*Moving Out of, or Not Living in, Attendance Areas of Closed Schools.* Some families that moved out of the attendance area of their closed school were turned away from enrolling into the district designated welcoming school because their new address fell outside of the attendance area boundary. Being turned away from a designated welcoming school also happened for families that did not move but were already living outside of the attendance area boundary of the closed school when the closing was announced. As one parent who lived outside of the attendance area of the closed school explained, *"...they didn't accept [her daughter] to go to the [designated welcoming school] because of the area we lived in."* Her daughter ultimately ended up attending her new neighborhood school, which happened to be a higher-rated school than the district designated welcoming school.

Not all families that were turned away from their designated welcoming school were able to enroll into higher-rated schools. As one mother whose children ended up in a school that was lower-rated than the designated welcoming school explained:

> I tried to enroll my children in two other schools before they were at their current school and neither one of the schools would accept my children, saying that they were out of the area, which I feel like it shouldn't have mattered if they were out of the area when you got this other school that is closing down.

Many of these families ended up at higher- or lower-rated schools simply by chance. In other words, their neighborhood school happened to be either a higher- or a lower-rated school than their designated welcoming school. One of these parents, when asked why she enrolled her son at their current higher-rated school, simply said that her family *"moved out of the neighborhood into another neighborhood, and [I sent] him to the neighborhood school."*

*Distance and Transportation Costs.* As we saw in the welcoming schools section, distance and transportation costs were barriers for many families. Figuring out how to get to and from school was a practical constraint that limited many parents' choice sets. The previous section showed that these constraints led parents to consider only the welcoming school. Likewise, many families that enrolled their children into other CPS schools were unable to consider enrolling in their designated welcoming schools for the same reasons—either the designated welcoming school was too far away or the cost of getting there every day was too great a burden.

Many of these families had either moved further away or already lived far from the designated welcoming school and felt that the longer commute to the welcoming school would be too far and unsafe for their children. For example, one parent said, *"…well he's gonna be on the bus, walking, you know, that, and with that being so unsafe, I just don't wanna chance it."* Her son ultimately ended up at a higher-rated neighborhood school closer to her home.

For families that originally did not live in the attendance area of the closed schools, or moved outside of the attendance areas of the closed school, many of the designated welcoming schools were much further away from their homes than their closed schools. Therefore, some schools were just too far away for parents to consider. One family member who enrolled her children into a lower-rated neighborhood school close to her new home explained:

> The staff notified me to let me know right then and there that you could send your children there [to the designated welcoming school], but they would not be bused there. That was a problem for me, because at the time I didn't have transportation, so I didn't have any means of getting them to the schools where I really desired for them to go. So I had to put them in a school that was a little closer to their neighborhood so they could be in walking distance of the school.

Access to transportation and the cost of transportation to and from welcoming schools was prohibitive for many of the families. Several parents said that because the district did not provide busing for their children to their designated welcoming schools, or help enough with public transportation funds, that they had to rule out the designated welcoming school because they could not afford it.

**Some families chose to enroll their children into other CPS schools because they better met their children's needs and family priorities than the designated welcoming school.** Although some families felt they did not have a choice—circumstances prevented the designated school from being an option—other families deliberately chose to send their children to another CPS school. Among families that felt they had a choice in schools, the primary reasons why families enrolled their children into their school differed considerably between those who chose a higher- vs. a lower-rated school.

**Overwhelmingly, families that chose to enroll into higher-rated CPS schools did so because of academic quality.** Almost all of the interviewees who enrolled into a school that was higher-rated than their assigned welcoming school said that school academic quality was the driving factor. Having high academic quality, however, meant different things to different parents. Most often, these families relied on *"official"* information gleaned from the district website, including test scores and test gains, performance policy ratings, high school acceptance rates, and attendance rates. Families wanted schools with higher academic quality so that their children would be challenged academically and progress in their schooling. One parent described her search process by saying:

> Well I went according to her grades and I picked it [the new school] due to their…, the stats, they had high numbers in their magnet school. She's really smart so that's how I picked it, according to their numbers. I looked on their website and just saw the different numbers—the attendance rate, parental involvement—like you can really get a breakdown of everything that goes on, so that's how I picked it.

In addition to the official academic markers described above, many of these parents/guardians also talked about wanting a school with small class sizes, which to them meant a better chance for their children to get individualized academic support and attention from teachers and other school staff. Prioritizing academics also meant that many families were attracted to particular types of schools or programs, such as magnet schools, language academies, International Baccalaureate (IB) programs, and STEM programs.

On the flip side, the most common reason why these families ruled out their designated welcoming schools was because they believed they were of lower academic quality. As one parent explained about her decision-making process:

> Neither one of them [the welcoming schools] could compare academically to what I was looking for my children, as far as like I said academic-wise. The thing is that academically, it [designated welcoming school] was not any different than [the closed school] in terms of like, ranking wise or grade point average wise, it wasn't any different. So if you close schools, why would I send my child out of [there] and send him to a school that you was just about to close, and that we were all at meetings together, and that is doing less well academically than what my child is at? No thanks. So that was a no.

Although low academic quality was the primary reason why these families shunned their designated welcoming schools, interviewees also mentioned other deterrents, including some safety concerns, hearing negative things about the welcoming schools from families and friends, and not wanting to send their children to any schools that were on potential closings lists.

**Overwhelmingly, families that enrolled in lower-rated CPS schools did so because of proximity to home.** The deciding factor for families that enrolled into schools that were lower-rated than their assigned welcoming school was the close proximity of the school to their home. Although these parents also talked about wanting schools that met their children's academic needs, distance was prioritized over other considerations—oftentimes because of safety concerns. Many families restricted their school search only to schools within a certain distance from their homes. As one family member stated, *"I had just really looked in the area that I live in and just seeing what school was the best option at that particular moment. Because I didn't have any idea on what school it was going to be."* Other families were not sure about the welcoming school, so they figured, *"Since they were going to be going to a new school anyway, you know, just have them stay in the neighborhood..."*

Additionally, several families in our sample moved the summer after the school closings announcement. These families were trying to navigate through their new neighborhoods and wanted to keep their children close. As previously discussed, parents often valued schools that were close in proximity to their homes, not only for convenience but also for practical considerations. These parents wanted to ensure that they could easily get to their children when needed. As one interviewee expressed it, *"I don't like putting my kids where it's far away from home, in case of unexpected—in case of weather."*

As mentioned above, safety also figured prominently in why parents wanted to keep their children close to home. The interviewee below discussed why she was against sending her child to the district designated welcoming school:

> Because—well, see I was against it because when you go in the route that we're supposed to be following just to get to that school, when you pass [a street] up in the middle of that, going to that school it's like a lot of 7-Elevens, a lot of people outside selling drugs....There's always shooting down there, and police are always down there with their lights, so, it's like, havoc.

Fear of gangs, drugs and drug dealers, guns, and violence were common concerns for parents who were worried about their children's safety as they commuted to new schools. Similar to families who opted for their designated welcoming schools, the distance from families' homes to the designated welcoming schools was linked with a sense of community within the neighborhood and safety concerns. For example, one parent said, *"But it's in gang territory and it's almost fifteen blocks from my house...And I wasn't going to send my son to anywhere like that."* These families believed that choosing a school close to their homes was the safer option, even if it meant sending their children to a school with lower test scores.

**Academics mattered for families that enrolled into lower-rated schools, but their definition of academic quality often differed from that of the district.** Although safety and proximity to home were the top considerations for families that ultimately enrolled into lower-rated schools, many of the interviewees also mentioned academic quality as a reason why they either ruled out their designated welcoming school or actively chose to enroll into their current schools. Even though their designated welcoming school was ranked higher the year that the schools closed, the way many parents defined academic quality did not match the district performance policy system. For instance, one parent worried that her children would go from a school where they were succeeding to one where they would languish:

> The school they wanted them to go to [designated welcoming school] was a low-functioning school. And I wasn't going to let them come out of that school where they had just excelled at, and go to a school where, you know, no acceleration there. I wasn't going to do that.

This parent decided to send her child to a much lower-rated school, but she felt that her child ultimately would do better academically in an environment that was different than the one the district assigned.

Academic quality for these families meant anything from schools having after-school programs, to having certain curricula and courses, small class sizes, and one-on-one attention from teachers in classes. In addition, several parents stressed the importance of enrolling their children into schools that were not overcrowded. One interviewee explained why this was important to her: *"I wanted them to get a better environment and to have a better chance of the teachers and the staff giving attention, you know, to their needs, being willing to help them."* This particular family chose a school that was only slightly lower-rated than their designated welcoming school. Many of these same parents expressed concern over larger class sizes at the welcoming schools and wondered whether their children would be able to get what they needed from their teachers.

Other family members prioritized giving their children opportunities to learn outside the classroom. For instance, one grandparent said that she was initially attracted to a school because of all the opportunities her granddaughter would have to keep busy with sports and enrichment programs. Additionally, some parents were focused on the name of the school or program and believed that *"academy," "magnet,"* or *"charter"* signified something meaningful about the academic quality of the school **(see the Vignette, *"Differing Definitions of Academic Quality Lead One Family to a Lower-Rated Magnet School"* on p.34)**. For example, one interviewee said he chose a different CPS school for the following reasons:

> Because it had changed into a language academy, and they also have a good academic program…the teaching and the learning process that they have. The many things that they teach the kids, like Spanish, different language and computer rooms, resources, you know, those types of things.

This particular school was significantly lower-rated than the district designated welcoming school.

Only a few of the families that enrolled into lower-rated schools talked about *"official"* markers of academic quality. Those that did sometimes recognized that the welcoming school did not have strong performance and might not be the best learning environment for their children. One interviewee, for example, spent time on the CPS website researching the designated welcoming school and perceived the school to be on a downward trajectory, noting that the school *"hasn't been really a good school since 2008, maybe, or 9. I think those are their highest test scores."* This welcoming school's policy points actually were on a downward trajectory over the years, and this parent noticed the trend. This family chose a school that was very comparable to their designated welcoming school but ranked slightly lower the year that the school closings were announced. Another parent was concerned with school probationary status of the welcoming school. She said:

> Well basically I was online looking through schools and researching their report cards and you know, probationary period and all that, you know. I did a thorough research before I made the decision that [their current charter school] was the best fit for my kids.

The charter school in which this parent enrolled her children was actually significantly lower-rated than the district designated welcoming school in terms of the performance policy points. However, the school had not existed long enough to have been assigned a performance level.

Overall, a very similar dichotomy emerges regarding choice vs. constraints among families that enrolled into district designated welcoming schools and families that enrolled into other CPS schools. Some families were able to exercise choice and picked schools they believed fit their family circumstances and priorities, while other families felt they had no choice and faced barriers getting into schools that they believed were better suited for their children. Families that deliberately enrolled into higher-rated schools prioritized official academic indicators when choosing schools for their children, although proximity to home and safety were also at the forefront. Those who deliberately enrolled in lower-rated schools prioritized proximity to home and safety; more often they used academic indicators that were unofficial instead of official.

## Factors that Mattered for Families Other than Location, Academics, and Safety

The displaced families we interviewed prioritized schools' academics, safety, and proximity to home, but they also valued and considered these other factors:

**Recommendations from Social Networks.** Some parents relied on their social networks for information about the quality of schools.

**Prior Experiences.** A few families had prior experiences with school staff or students and either strongly considered or ruled out schools based on these prior experiences.

**Personal Connection to Schools.** Simply knowing about a school through a personal or family connection often put that school into consideration.

**Special Education Supports.** Some children needed very specific kinds of supports or programs that were not offered at every school, and many of these families had to actively look for schools that met their children's needs.

**Juggling Multiple Children's Needs.** Families with multiple children had more complicated choice sets because these families often prioritized keeping their children together, and they tried to find one school to meet all of their children's needs.

**Affordability of Fees.** A few families had to rule out charter and private schools they were considering because they could not afford the fees. They also cited uniforms or other costs.

**Racial Composition of Schools.** Some parents wanted their children to move to a more racially diverse school because they wanted their children to be exposed to multiple cultures. Others ruled out some schools if they believed their child would in the racial minority.

**Safety and Security Within Schools.** Parents not only wanted their children to have a safe commute to and from school, but they also wanted them to feel safe while at school. For example, many families talked about wanting strict discipline practices and clear safety measures.

MRS. EDWARDS: A VIGNETTE

# Differing Definitions of Academic Quality Lead One Family to a Lower-Rated Magnet School

Mrs. Edwards (a pseudonym) has two young children. Her son was in kindergarten and her daughter was in second grade when it was announced their elementary school would close. Mrs. Edwards stressed that she liked everything about the closed school. She liked the teachers because they emphasized responsibility in their classrooms and she appreciated that the office staff treated everyone equally.

Mrs. Edwards found everyone to be very welcoming and responsive to her and her children. This was especially important to her because she is a self-proclaimed *"foreigner."* She explained:

> ...these kids came in with accents. And sometimes they [school staff] don't really understand [the children]. Both of them speak English from home; they understand English perfectly well, but the accents... they're in a new environment. Even though they came in new, they accepted them wholeheartedly, and they treat them nice.

The Edwards family immigrated to the United States the year the closings were announced. They had enrolled at their neighborhood school in December, after lists of potential closings had been released and rumors of closings were circulating. Right away, Mrs. Edwards began to search for new schools, applying to over 20 magnet and selective enrollment elementary schools and programs. She believes if you want your children to go to college, then they must be in magnet or selective enrollment programs. In her words:

> Because I have this general belief that magnet schools are good schools. They are much better than neighborhood schools or open enrollment schools. Because you just don't get admission into magnet schools.

Despite applying to over 20 schools before the official closings announcement, both Edwards children were offered admission to only one magnet school. Mrs. Edwards describes the school as *"still not good."* But keeping the children together and getting them out of a traditional neighborhood school were priorities.

Mrs. Edwards did not seriously consider sending her children to their designated welcoming school for several reasons. Strong academics were important and she did not believe the welcoming school was a good option. She explained, *"I can't take my kids there. I can't take my kids to Level 3—from Level 3 to Level 3."* She also prioritized smaller class sizes and schools, saying, *"I didn't pick [the welcoming school] because they're highly populated."* Distance from home also drove her decision: The designated welcoming school was not within walking distance, whereas the school she selected was much closer.

Though the magnet school her children were admitted to was lower-rated than the designated welcoming school, in Mrs. Edwards' opinion it was a better school for her children. To her, the word "magnet" meant strong academic performance—even though the test scores and performance policy ranking did not reflect that.

# CHAPTER 4

# Interpretive Summary

While school closures may have potentially positive financial and academic effects, they are inevitably disruptive and burdensome for families and communities. This is particularly true in a "choice" system, where families may opt to send their children to schools outside of their attendance area boundary.

In such systems, when schools close, families by definition are faced with a forced transition to a new school. How districts guide and support families through the process—deciding on a new school and transitioning—can determine the success or failure of the policy. The theory underlying CPS's closing strategy was that students would do better if they moved to higher-performing schools. To maximize the likelihood that students would attend better schools, CPS assigned students to higher-rated welcoming schools, invested additional resources in the welcoming schools, provided families with information about their school options, and offered some level of support around safe passage to new schools. Ultimately, two-thirds of families followed the district's plan for them by attending the welcoming school to which they were assigned. Another one-third opted for different schools—often attending schools that were lower-rated than their assigned welcoming school. How this reshuffling played out offers important lessons for other districts considering closing schools—and, more broadly, for all districts operating within a choice system.

**A choice policy predicated on sending students to higher-performing schools is constrained by the availability of high-quality seats.** While the CPS policy did succeed in sending the vast majority of students to schools that were more highly-rated than their closed schools, only 21 percent managed to attend a Level 1 school.[31] This is potentially problematic because past research found that students' achievement improved only if they moved to a substantially higher-performing school than the one they left.[32] Though CPS assigned all students to a higher-rated school, just 27 percent were assigned to a Level 1 school (the district's highest rating). Meanwhile, 30 percent were assigned to a Level 3 school (the district's lowest rating). This suggests that there were simply not enough available seats in higher-rated schools in these neighborhoods to accommodate all of the displaced students. In cases where families lived in neighborhoods with few high-rated schools and limited transportation options, they had a harder time attending higher-rated schools. Without strong schools in these neighborhoods or access to affordable transportation, the goal of sending students to better-performing schools might be hard to achieve.

---

[31] Prior to the school closures, none of the displaced students attended Level 1 schools.
[32] de la Torre & Gwynne (2009); Engberg et al. (2012).

**What may appear to be a "poor choice" based solely on performance policy ratings may, in fact, be a nuanced choice by families based on the needs of their children.** Two-thirds of those students who did not attend their designated welcoming school attended schools with lower-performance policy points than their assigned welcoming school. Some may interpret this finding as a failure on the part of parents/guardians by suggesting they did not make *"good"* academic choices.[33] However, the majority of families we spoke to chose schools based on other factors that they thought would better fit their children's needs. The majority of interviewees also put a lot of thought and effort into finding the right schools for their children.

When deciding on schools, families think about a range of school characteristics that may meet their individual children's learning needs. Some families said that the assigned welcoming schools did not meet their children's needs—in these cases, it is appropriate to question whether the district's performance policy rating system is the best rubric by which to judge school quality for every student. Some students may fare better in schools with a more supportive environment, for example, or with a more robust arts program, or with more active parent involvement. Of course, these qualities are not mutually exclusive of strong test scores—a high-ranking school, for example, may also have a renowned music program—but the performance policy rubric would capture only one dimension of that school's strengths.

**Confidence in children's safety trumps many other things that schools might be able to offer.** Children's safety was a big concern for families, not only inside the school building but also for their children's commute to and from school. If children's safety is key for families, can something be done to help them feel that schools (other than the nearby school) are safe choices? The Safe Passage program helped some families feel safe on the way to the new school. But for other families, it was not enough. Families often addressed the issue of safety by keeping children in a nearby school. This meant that some students attended higher- or lower-rated schools simply because of where they lived.

Access to transportation may help alleviate some safety concerns, and some families may benefit from help with logistical issues and financial burdens. Working with communities and families to develop a tailored neighborhood safe passage plan may also help.

**Many of the families we interviewed simply felt overwhelmed and without the support they needed to make informed decisions on a critical aspect of their children's lives—a new school.** Two issues contributed to this: The information they received from the district and from other sources and the timing of the school closings decisions. As mentioned in Chapter 1, the district sent families multiple written forms of communication—transition plans and letters—and made these documents available on their website. However, some families said they never received the information. For other families that successfully received the information, it appears that the critical components—such as the name of the designated welcoming school, the fact that families had other options, or enrollment dates—did not come across as clearly and accurately as families needed. This confusion is not surprising, given the amount of information sent to parents in a very short period of time. Moreover, the information provided about the designated welcoming schools was inconsistent—some, but not all, welcoming schools provided detailed information about program offerings and academic support plans for students. In other words, different families received different kinds and amounts of information. For many families, the information proved overwhelming and/or unclear.

Although CPS produced a plethora of written information about the designated welcoming schools, they did not supply information directly about other schools in the district. Some families did receive information about other schools near their closed school (some school staff put together information packets for families), or by attending open-enrollment fairs or by using the *"find a school"* application on the CPS website. However, families said they wished they had received more digestible information in multiple formats (written and verbal) about all of their available school options.

---

[33] Asimov (2003); Holme (2002).

**Families we interviewed said they wished they had more time to research available options and make informed decisions.** Many parents/guardians felt that CPS failed to provide them with the time required to make such a complex and important decision as finding a new school for their children. With more time and the ability to participate in the regular application process, families would have felt less pressured processing the details and options that CPS provided. Prior research has shown that the most negative impact of school closings, as measured by reading and math test scores, occurs the year of the closings announcement.[34] Normally, announcements on school closings are required to take place by December 1. CPS was granted an extension until the end of March in order to have *"an extensive community engagement process."* In addition, CEO Barbara Byrd-Bennett said that extending the deadline would allow schools to concentrate on preparing students for the annual ISAT tests at the beginning of March.[35] However, the delay in the announcement had repercussions for the families affected by closings. They reported wishing that the district had made the decision earlier and given their family more time, which would have allowed them to deal with the emotional toll of losing their school community and prepare to make a transition. Families also said that if they had more time they could have researched and gathered more information about other school options for their children—schools that might have better met their children's needs. Families said they could have visited more schools they were considering and better worked through the logistics they needed to figure out how to send their children to the school they wanted. Additionally, families could have applied to schools and programs that require applications and or lotteries for acceptance. Sticking to the December deadline certainly would have given families more time—almost six more months—and it might have provided them with the necessary time to research more options for their children and to apply to the schools and programs within application deadlines.

**Families with children who have IEPs faced particular challenges in finding schools with the necessary supports and services for their children.** As we illustrated in this report, the closed schools served more vulnerable students than the district average—in particular, these schools were more likely to have served students with IEPs. In fact, one-third of closed schools had special education cluster programs. These cluster programs, which were more likely to have been in underutilized schools, provided services to children with serious disabilities. In our interviews, the parents of children with special needs and/or IEPs prioritized the special needs of their child. They wanted their children to get the supports they needed to learn and grow, and they wanted their children to be in close proximity to their homes. But these parents had limited information on how the designated welcoming schools would serve their children. The transition letters stated simply that their children would receive the same supports at the welcoming schools, and that someone from CPS would contact them to talk about the welcoming schools and answer questions. The transition plans also stated that CPS would provide network offices with additional resources to work directly with families to explain school options. In some cases, families realized that the supports at the designated welcoming school were not adequate and had to look for other schools in the district to meet their children's needs. Giving parents more information about how these schools would serve their children and more time to digest that information, research on their own, and prepare their children for a school transition, might have helped these parents/guardians enroll their children in schools that met their childrens' specific needs.

---

When closing schools, trying to send students to better-performing schools is a sensible goal; it is consistent with research on what matters for improving learning. It is important to consider in a "choice" system, however, that families value many school characteristics in addition to test scores when deciding where to enroll their children. In an ideal setting, families would be able to choose from any school in the district that meets

---

34 de la Torre & Gwynne (2009); Barrow et al. (2011).

35 Ahmed-Ullah (2012, November 2).

their children's needs. In reality, however, the choice sets for families are limited by practical constraints—where they live, budgetary limitations, the availability of transportation, the number of *"good"* options in their neighborhood, etc.[36] These mitigating factors make it more difficult for some families to enroll into better schools. In some cases, constraints and barriers leave families with no choice or agency in the process at all. As other districts look to shape closing policies that will at once save money and optimize student learning, it is imperative to understand the mechanisms that facilitate or constrain families from enrolling their children in higher-performing schools that also meet their needs.

More research is needed to examine how the transition year went for families and students. It is important to investigate how affected students do academically, socially, and behaviorally in their new school settings and to unpack which school characteristics matter most for improving student outcomes. Lastly, not much is known about how closing schools affects teachers and other staff or the impact closing schools has on the composition of the entire school staff. Cultivating a better understanding of the impact of closing schools on families, students, and school staff could help districts facilitate better educational experiences and student outcomes in the future.

---

[36] For more information about the concept of *"choice-sets"* see Bell (2007 and 2009).

# References

Ahmed-Ullah, N. (2012, November 2). CPS wants more time to compile school closing list. *Chicago Tribune*. Retrieved from http://articles.chicagotribune.com/2012-11-02/news/chi-cps-wants-more-time-to-compile-school-closing-list-20121102_1_school-closings-school-actions-cps-officials

Ahmed-Ullah, N. (2012, December 5). CPS lists 330 underutilized schools. *Chicago Tribune*. Retrieved from http://articles.chicagotribune.com/2012-12-05/news/chi-board-of-education-releases-enrollment-schooluse-figures-20121204_1_ceo-barbara-byrd-bennett-school-closings-charter-schools

Ahmed-Ullah, N. (2013, April 15). At Chicago school closing hearings, crowds fade. *Chicago Tribune*. Retrieved from http://articles.chicagotribune.com/2013-04-25/news/ct-met-cps-closing-hearings-20130426_1_schools-chief-barbara-byrd-bennett-final-list-two-community-meetings

Ahmed-Ullah, N. (2013, August 9). CPS releases maps of 'safe passage' routes. *Chicago Tribune*. Retrieved from http://articles.chicagotribune.com/2013-08-09/news/chi-cps-releases-maps-of-safe-passage-routes-20130809_1_safe-passage-program-ceo-barbara-byrd-bennett-rival-gang-territories

Asimov, N. (2003, October 9). Few parents seize chance to transfer schools 'No Child Left Behind' made offer mandatory. *The San Francisco Chronicle*, p. A1.

Barrow, L., Park, K., & Schanzenbach, D.W. (2011). *Assessing the impacts on students of closing persistently failing schools*. Working Paper.

Bell, C.A. (2007). Space and place: Urban parents' geographical preferences for schools. *The Urban Review, 39*(4), 375-404.

Bell, C.A. (2009). All choices created equal? The role of choice sets in the selection of schools. *Peabody Journal of Education, 84*(2), 191-208.

Brummet, Q. (2014). The effects of school closings on student achievement. *Journal of Public Economics, 119,* 108-124.

Chicago Public Schools. (2012). *2012-2013 Guidelines for school actions*. Retrieved from http://www.cps.edu/ABOUT_CPS/POLICIES_AND_GUIDELINES/Pages/2013GuidelinesforSchoolActions.aspx

Chicago Public Schools. (2012, October 12). *Mayor Emanuel names Barbara Byrd-Bennett new CEO*. Retrieved from http://www.cps.edu/spotlight/pages/Spotlight362.aspx

Chicago Public Schools. (2012, October 31). *CPS releases draft school actions guidelines that integrate community feedback*. Retrieved from http://cps.edu/News/Press_releases/Pages/10_31_2012_PR1.aspx

Chicago Public Schools. (2012, November 2). *CPS CEO Barbara Byrd-Bennett to launch thorough community engagement process on school actions*. Retrieved from http://cps.edu/News/Press_releases/Pages/11_02_2012_PR1.aspx

Chicago Public Schools. (2012, November 26). *CPS announces five-year moratorium on facility closures starting in fall 2013*. Retrieved from http://cps.edu/News/Press_releases/Pages/11_26_2012_PR1.aspx

Chicago Public Schools. (2012, December 11). *CPS reminds families to explore academic offerings as application process deadline approaches*. Retrieved from http://cps.edu/News/Press_releases/Pages/12_11_2012_PR1.aspx

Chicago Public Schools. (2013, January 10). *Statement from CEO Barbara Byrd-Bennett on release of commission on school utilization report*. Retrieved from http://cps.edu/News/Press_releases/Pages/01_10_2013_PR1.aspx

Chicago Public Schools. (2013, January 11). *CEO Barbara Byrd-Bennett announces 2nd round of community engagement on school utilization*. Retrieved from http://cps.edu/News/Press_releases/Pages/01_11_2013_PR1.aspx

Chicago Public Schools. (2013, February 13). *Based on community feedback, CPS releases detailed criteria to help guide decisions on district's utilization crisis*. Retrieved from http://cps.edu/News/Press_releases/Pages/2_13_2013_PR1.aspx

Chicago Public Schools. (2013, March 14). *CPS outlines comprehensive student safety transition plan*. Retrieved from http://cps.edu/News/Press_releases/Pages/3_14_2013_PR1.aspx

Chicago Public Schools. (2013a, March 21). *Media briefing*. Retrieved from https://cbschicago.files.wordpress.com/2013/03/cps-briefing.pdf.

Chicago Public Schools. (2013b, March 21). *CPS CEO Byrd-Bennett announces nearly twenty new IB, STEM and fine arts programs will roll out in welcoming schools next fall.* Retrieved from http://cps.edu/News/Press_releases/Pages/3_21_2013_PR1.aspx

Chicago Public Schools. (2013c, March 21). *Significant new investments to provide quality, 21st century education for CPS students transitioning from underutilized schools this fall.* Retrieved from http://cps.edu/News/Press_releases/Pages/3_21_2013_PR2.aspx

Chicago Public Schools. (2013, April 3). *Third phase of community meetings around CPS school utilization begins this Saturday.* Retrieved from http://cps.edu/News/Press_releases/Pages/4_3_2013_PR1.aspx

Chicago Public Schools. (2013, April 15). *Public hearings on consolidating underutilized schools and other actions begin Tuesday.* Retrieved from http://cps.edu/News/Press_releases/Pages/4_15_2013_PR1.aspx

Chicago Public Schools. (2013, April 29). *Public hearings on consolidating underutilized schools and other actions continue this week.* Retrieved from http://cps.edu/News/Press_releases/Pages/4_29_2013_PR1.aspx

Chicago Public Schools. (2013, May 20). *CPS releases updated draft transition plans to address specific issues identified in hearing officer reports.* Retrieved from http://www.cps.edu/News/Press_Releases/Pages/PR1_05_20_2013.aspx

Chicago Public Schools. (2013, May 22). *Nearly 50 percent of students at sending schools enroll early for SY 13-14.* Retrieved from http://cps.edu/News/Press_releases/Pages/PR_05_30_2013.aspx

Chicago Public Schools. (2013, May 30). *Chicago board of education votes to consolidate underutilized, under-resourced schools.* Retrieved from http://cps.edu/News/Press_releases/Pages/PR1_5_22_2013.aspx

Chicago Public Schools. (2013, June 3). *Parents enroll 78 percent of students during early enrollment for new schools.* Retrieved from http://cps.edu/News/Press_releases/Pages/PR1_06_03_2013.aspx

Chicago Public Schools. (2013, July 12). *Transition plan as of July 12, 2013, for the closure of John P. Altgeld Elementary School.* Retrieved from http://schoolinfo.cps.edu/SchoolActions/Download.aspx?fid=2952

de la Torre, M., & Gwynne, J. (2009). *When schools close: Effects on displaced students in Chicago Public Schools.* Chicago, IL: University of Chicago Consortium on Chicago School Research.

Duncan, A. (2009, June 30). *Turning around the bottom five percent.* Washington, DC: National Alliance for Public Charter Schools Conference

Engberg, J., Gill, B., Zamarro, G., & Zimmer, R. (2012). Closing schools in a shrinking district: Do student outcomes depend on which schools are closed? *Journal of Urban Economics, 71*(2), 189-203.

Hastings, J.S., Kane, T.J., & Staiger, D.O. (2005). *Parental preferences and school competition: Evidence from a public school choice program* (No. w11805). Washington, DC: National Bureau of Economic Research.

Holme J.J. (2002). Buying homes, buying schools: School choice and the social construction of school quality. *Harvard Educational Review, 72*(2), 177-207.

Illinois Board of Education. (2013). *2013 Illinois State Assessments.* Retrieved from http://www.isbe.net/assessment/pdfs/Chart2013.pdf

Karp, S. (2013, November 21). After closings, questions linger on special ed programs. *Catalyst Chicago.* Retrieved from http://www.catalyst-chicago.org/news/

Kirshner, B., Gaertner, M., & Pozzoboni, K. (2010). Tracing transitions: The effect of high school closure on displaced students. *Educational Evaluation and Policy Analysis, 32*(3), 407–429.

Lutton, L., & Vevea, B. (2013, March 21). Chicago proposes closing 53 elementary schools, firing staff at another 6. *WBEZ.* Retrieved from http://www.wbez.org/news/chicago-proposes-closing-53-elementary-schools-firing-staff-another-6-106202

New Hope Community Service Center. (n.d.). *About safe passage.* Retrieved from http://www.nhcsc.org/safe.html

Patton, M.Q. (2002). *Qualitative research & evaluation methods* (2nd ed.). Thousand Oaks, CA: Sage Publications, Inc.

Rothstein, J. (2004). *Good principals or good peers? Parental valuation of school characteristics, Tiebout equilibrium, and the effects of inter-district competition* (No. w10666). Washington, DC: National Bureau of Economic Research.

Sikkink, D., & Emerson, M.O. (2008). School choice and racial segregation in US schools: The role of parents' education. *Ethnic and Racial Studies, 31*(2), 267-293.

Tedin, K.L., & Weiher, G.R. (2004). Racial/ethnic diversity and academic quality as components of school choice. *Journal of Politics, 66*(4), 1109-1133.

# Appendix A
## Closed Schools and Designated Welcoming Schools

**Table A.1** shows the 47 closed schools and their designated welcoming schools. It also offers information on their utilization rates, performance data, and other characteristics related to the process of determining which schools were closed and which were designated as welcoming schools. Numbers in darker shaded columns refer to welcoming schools.

**TABLE A.1**

**Characteristics of Closed Schools, Designated Welcoming Schools, and Other Information**

| Closed School | Welcoming School(s) | Utilization Rate | | 2012-13 Performance Level | | Other Information |
|---|---|---|---|---|---|---|
| Altgeld | Wentworth | 48% | 41% | Level 3 (26%) | Level 3 (45%) | Wentworth moved to the location of Altgeld. Bond's attendance area was redrawn to accommodate part of Altgeld's attendance area. New STEM program at Wentworth. Transportation provided for current Wentworth students to new Wentworth location. |
| Armstrong | Leland | 36% | 81% | Level 2 (62%) | Level 1 (93%) | Leland moved to a new location (at Mays' old location). New STEM program at Leland. |
| Banneker | Mays | 49% | 64% | Level 3 (43%) | Level 3 (45%) | Mays moved to the location of Banneker. |
| Bethune | Gregory | 48% | 37% | Level 3 (36%) | Level 1 (81%) | Jensen's attendance area was redrawn to accommodate part of Bethune's attendance area. Transportation provided for students welcomed at Gregory. |
| Bontemps | Nicholson | 46% | 50% | Level 3 (17%) | Level 1 (81%) | New STEM program at Nicholson. Transportation provided for students welcomed at Nicholson. |
| Buckingham | Montefiore | 54% | 13% | Level 3 (31%) | Level 3 (39%) | Transportation provided for those who received transportation at Buckingham. Current Buckingham students with bus aides based on IEPs have this support continued. Montefiore's attendance was redrawn to accommodate students from Near North. |
| Calhoun | Cather | 46% | 30% | Level 2 (69%) | Level 1 (76%) | |
| Delano | Melody | 37% | 34% | Level 2 (55%) | Level 2 (62%) | Melody moved to the location of Delano. Hefferan's attendance area was redrawn to accommodate part of Melody's attendance area. Transportation provided for current Melody students to new Melody location, to be reevaluated after the 2013-14 school year. |
| Dumas | Wadsworth | 36% | 46% | Level 3 (26%) | Level 3 (45%) | Wadsworth moved to the location of Dumas. New STEM program at Wadsworth. |
| Duprey | De Diego | 28% | 71% | Level 2 (50%) | Level 2 (57%) | New IB program at De Diego. |
| Emmet | DePriest | 66% | 61% | Level 3 (48%) | Level 2 (57%) | New IB program at DePriest and Ellington. |
| | Ellington | | 43% | | Level 1 (71%) | |
| Fermi | South Shore | 53% | 79% | Level 3 (24%) | Level 3 (44%) | Wadsworth's attendance area was redrawn to accommodate part of Fermi's attendance area. |

Appendix A

**TABLE A.1:** *CONTINUED*

**Characteristics of Closed Schools, Designated Welcoming Schools, and Other Information**

| Closed School | Welcoming School(s) | Utilization Rate | | 2012-13 Performance Level | | Other Information |
|---|---|---|---|---|---|---|
| Garfield Park | Faraday | 39% | 47% | Level 3 (17%) | Level 1 (74%) | |
| Goldblatt | Hefferan | 30% | 40% | Level 2 (69%) | Level 1 (74%) | New STEM program at Hefferan. |
| Goodlow | Earle | 60% | 43% | Level 3 (31%) | Level 3 (36%) | Earle moved to the location of Goodlow. O'Toole's and Bass' attendance areas were redrawn to accommodate part of Earle's attendance area. New STEM program at Earle. |
| Henson | C. Hughes | 32% | 56% | Level 3 (10%) | Level 2 (57%) | Herzl's and Webster's attendance areas were redrawn to accommodate part of Henson's attendance area. |
| Herbert | Dett | 44% | 25% | Level 3 (38%) | Level 2 (52%) | Dett moved to the location of Herbert. Cather's attendance area was redrawn to accommodate part of Dett's attendance area |
| Key | Ellington | 57% | 43% | Level 2 (50%) | Level 1 (71%) | New IB program at Ellington. |
| King | Jensen | 43% | 45% | Level 3 (33%) | Level 1 (83%) | Transportation provided for students welcomed at Jensen. |
| Kohn | Lavizzo | 37% | 61% | Level 3 (36%) | Level 1 (71%) | New STEM program at L. Hughes. Transportation provided for students welcomed at Cullen. |
| | L. Hughes | | 48% | | Level 3 (48%) | |
| | Cullen | | 68% | | Level 2 (67%) | |
| Lafayette | Chopin | 36% | 37% | Level 3 (26%) | Level 1 (76%) | |
| Lawrence | Burnham | 47% | 89% | Level 3 (36%) | Level 2 (55%) | Burnham moved to the location of Lawrence. |
| Marconi | Tilton | 41% | 39% | Level 3 (43%) | Level 2 (50%) | New STEM program at Tilton. |
| May | Leland | 45% | 81% | Level 3 (45%) | Level 1 (93%) | Leland moved to the location of May. Leland's attendance boundaries redrawn to also accommodate part of Armstrong's attendance area. New STEM program and curriculum at Leland. |
| Mayo | Wells | 59% | 51% | Level 3 (26%) | Level 3 (26%) | Wells moved to the location of Mayo. New IB program at Wells. |
| Morgan | Ryder | 31% | 44% | Level 3 (33%) | Level 3 (36%) | Gresham's and Wescott's attendance areas were redrawn to accommodate part of Morgan's attendance area. |
| Near North | Montefiore | 53% | 13% | Level 3 (17%) | Level 3 (39%) | All Near North students received transportation and continued to receive transportation to Montefiore. All current Near North students with bus aides based on IEPs continued to receive that support. |
| Overton | Mollison | 51% | 44% | Level 3 (36%) | Level 3 (48%) | Burke's attendance area was redrawn to accommodate part of Overton's attendance area. Transportation provided for students welcomed at Mollison. New IB program at Mollison. |
| Owens | Gompers | 68% | 55% | Level 3 (27%) | Level 3 (43%) | New STEM program at Gompers. |

**TABLE A.1:** *CONTINUED*

**Characteristics of Closed Schools, Designated Welcoming Schools, and Other Information**

| Closed School | Welcoming School(s) | Utilization Rate | 2012-13 Performance Level | | Other Information |
|---|---|---|---|---|---|
| Paderewski | Cardenas | 30% | 84% | Level 3 (45%) | Level 1 (77%) | Penn's and Crown's attendance areas were redrawn to accommodate part of Paderewski's attendance area. |
| | Castellanos | | 91% | | Level 2 (52%) | |
| Parkman | Sherwood | 41% | 55% | Level 3 (45%) | Level 2 (52%) | Transportation provided for students welcomed at Sherwood, service to be reevaluated after 2013-14 school year. |
| Peabody | Otis | 47% | 60% | Level 3 (48%) | Level 2 (69%) | |
| Pershing West | Pershing East | 27% | 92% | Level 2 (52%) | Level 2 (60%) | Pershing East moved to the location of Pershing West. |
| Pope | Johnson | 34% | 58% | Level 3 (45%) | Level 2 (67%) | |
| Ross | Dulles | 37% | 61% | Level 3 (31%) | Level 2 (64%) | New pre-K program at Dulles. |
| Ryerson | Ward, L | 58% | 55% | Level 2 (50%) | Level 2 (64%) | Ward moved to the location of Ryerson. New STEM program at Ward. |
| Sexton | Fiske | 41% | 41% | Level 2 (50%) | Level 2 (64%) | Fiske moved to the location of Sexton. New IB program at Fiske. |
| Songhai | Curtis | 44% | 53% | Level 3 (33%) | Level 2 (52%) | |
| Stewart | Brennemann | 41% | 51% | Level 2 (64%) | Level 2 (67%) | |
| Stockton | Courtenay | 45% | 85% | Level 3 (38%) | Level 2 (64%) | Courtenay moved to the location of Stockton. |
| Trumbull | Chappell | 54% | 71% | Level 3 (43%) | Level 1 (88%) | Peirce's attendance area was also redrawn to accommodate part of Trumbull's attendance area. Transportation provided for students welcomed at McPherson and McCutcheon. |
| | McPherson | | 63% | | Level 2 (57%) | |
| | McCutcheon | | 89% | | Level 2 (67%) | |
| Von Humboldt | De Diego | 40% | 71% | Level 2 (50%) | Level 2 (57%) | New IB program at De Diego. |
| West Pullman | Haley | 44% | 61% | Level 3 (31%) | Level 2 (55%) | Metcalfe's attendance area was redrawn to accommodate part of West Pullman's attendance area. Transportation provided for students welcomed at Haley, service to be reevaluated after the 2013-14 school year. New Fine and Performing Arts program at Haley. |
| Williams ES | Drake | 66% | 35% | Level 3 (26%) | Level 3 (43%) | Drake moved to the location of Williams. |
| Williams MS | Drake | 53% | 35% | Level 3 (21%) | Level 3 (43%) | Drake moved to the location of Williams and co-located with Urban Prep. |
| Woods | Bass | 46% | 41% | Level 3 (43%) | Level 2 (60%) | Langford's and Nicholson's attendance areas were redrawn to accommodate part of Woods' attendance area. |
| Yale | Harvard | 27% | 70% | Level 3 (29%) | Level 3 (43%) | New pre-K program at Harvard. |

Appendix A

# Appendix B
Quantitative Data, Sample, and Analyses

## Data

Data for the analysis come from CPS administrative records, including information on demographics, students' residential address, school enrollment, and test scores; surveys about students' school experiences, neighborhood crime reports from the Chicago Police Department, and data on neighborhoods from the U.S. Census at the block group level. All of these data sources are linked together using a unique student identifier, with crime and census data linked to each student's home address.

**TABLE B.1**

**Description of Variables**

| | |
|---|---|
| **Student Variables** | Demographic variables such as gender, race/ethnicity, special education status, limited English proficiency, old for grade (suggesting the student has been retained), attending attendance area school, and change in residences (it is not possible to calculate residential mobility for every student; we create a variable with three possible values: moved, did not move, no data) |
| **Neighborhood Characteristics** | Student addresses allow for linking of students to their census block group characteristics. We use two socio-economic metrics based on these block groups. The first is a measure of **concentration of poverty** in the census block group and includes the percent of adult males unemployed and the percent of families with incomes below the poverty line. The second is a measure of **social status** in the census block group and includes the mean level of education of adults and the percentage of employed persons who work as managers or professionals. These measures are created from the 2000 Census (for the 2008 and 2009 cohorts) and from the American Community Survey (for the 2010 and 2011 cohorts). <br><br> **An indicator based on Chicago Police Department incident statistics provided by address, and is calculated as the log of the crime rate, where the crime rate is the ratio of total number of crimes to the total population by census block. Crime data are updated for each year.** |
| **Test Scores** | Student performance on the Illinois Standards Achievement Test (ISAT) in math. Scores are standardized within grade and then 5 groups are formed, based on quintiles, well below-average, below-average, average, above-average and well below-average. The majority of students in grades 3 through 8 take this test. |
| **Safety** | Rasch scale made from the items students answered in My Voice, My School survey and then aggregated to the school level. <br> **How Safe Do You Feel…** <br> • Outside around the school? <br> • Traveling between home and school? <br> • In the hallways and bathrooms of the school? <br> • In your class? <br> (Possible answers: Not Safe, Somewhat Safe, Mostly Safe, Very Safe) |
| **Distance** | Shortest distance from geocoded students' addresses to geocoded schools' addresses |
| **Other School Options Within 1/2 Mile** | Number of CPS elementary schools within a radius of 1/2 mile of a student's residence. |

## Sample

There were 13,878 students enrolled in the 47 closed schools at the end of May 2013. These schools were serving students from pre-kindergarten to eighth grade. For our study, we followed students in elementary grades who had to reenroll in elementary grades—basically students in kindergarten through seventh grade—to understand where they attended school in the fall of 2013. This is a group of 10,708 students.[37] Almost all students who were in eighth grade in May 2013 enrolled in CPS high schools. The rest were young children enrolled in pre-kindergarten. **Table B.2** shows the characteristics of these students, as well as of all CPS students and students attending the 129 elementary schools that were considered for closing earlier in the year. The 47 schools that eventually closed were on that list.

**TABLE B.2**

Characteristics of K-7 Student Population Enrolled in CPS Schools in May 2013

|  | Students Enrolled in 47 Closed Elementary Schools (10,708 students) | Students Enrolled in 129 Elementary Schools Initially Considered for Closure (33,564 students) | All K-7 CPS Students (235,067 students) |
|---|---|---|---|
| Percent African American | 88% | 88% | 39% |
| Percent Latino | 10% | 10% | 46% |
| Percent White | 1% | 1% | 10% |
| Percent Receiving Special Education Services | 17% | 16% | 13% |
| Percent English Language Learners | 5% | 5% | 21% |
| Percent Receiving Free or Reduced-Price Lunch | 95% | 94% | 85% |
| Percent Old for Grade | 16% | 16% | 8% |
| ISAT Math (% meeting/exceeding standards-Spring 12) | 29% | 29% | 47% |
| Percent with Missing Test Score Data | 53% | 54% | 54% |
| Percent Living in Attendance Area of School | 64% | 64% | 63% |
| Percent Changed Residences (May 2012-September 2012) | 14% | 12% | 7% |
| Percent Changed Schools (May 2012-September 2012) | 24% | 23% | 21% |
| Crime Rate in Students' Neighborhoods (rate per 100 people) | 23 | 22 | 13 |
| Percent Males in Students' Neighborhood Who are Employed | 60% | 60% | 75% |

[37] Among the students in our sample, there are some ungraded special education students for whom it is not appropriate to be in a particular grade, who were older than four years by September 2012.

## Quantitative Analyses

### Reenrolling in the District

We used data for the three years prior to the school closings— 2010, 2011, and 2012—and 2013, the year of closing. The population in the analysis is based on students enrolled in grades K-7 in CPS schools in May of those years. We created a variable coded 1 if students reenrolled in any CPS school in the fall of that year, 0 otherwise. That is the dependent variable in the analysis. We ran a logistic regression model with school fixed-effects and a dummy variable representing the observations in the year 2013 to capture the difference in the reenrollment rates in 2013 compared to the prior three years for each school. We also used a dummy variable for whether the student was enrolled in a closed school to compare the changes in district reenrollment in other CPS schools and the 47 schools affected by the closures. We ran the model with no controls for student characteristics and again with such controls in case the student population in the schools had changed over time and could account for any differences. We clustered the standard errors to account for the nesting of students within schools.

Table B.3 shows the estimates and p-values produced by this model. The positive coefficient for the 2013 year dummy variable indicates that students were more likely to reenroll in CPS schools in the fall of 2013 than in previous years. The negative estimate on the cross product of 2013 and the dummy variable for the closed schools indicates that the students in these schools were less likely to reenroll in CPS than students in other schools, but the difference is not statistically significant. These results suggest that students did not leave the district at higher rates after the schools closed.

### Enrolling in the Designated Welcoming School

The sample of students for this analysis was based on the 10,062 displaced students who reenrolled in a CPS school in the fall of 2013. The dependent variable in this analysis was coded as 1 when a student enrolled in the designated welcoming school, 0 otherwise. We included in the model variables about student characteristics, their neighborhood, and the designated welcoming school. We used a logistic regression and clustered the standard errors on the 53 clusters formed by the closed schools and their respective designated welcoming schools (43 closed schools were assigned one welcoming school, two closed schools had two welcoming schools and two closed schools had three welcoming schools assigned to them). Table B.4 shows the results of the estimation.

**TABLE B.3**

**Analyses of CPS Reenrollment Rates: Logistic Regressions With Fixed Effects and Clustered Standard Errors at the School Level (p-values in parentheses)**

|  | Logistic Regression | |
|---|---|---|
|  | With No Student Controls | With Student Controls |
| Dummy variable for 2013 | 0.145 (<.00010) | 0.163 (<.00010) |
| Dummy variable 2013 x Dummy for Closed School | -0.138 (0.07) | -0.138 (0.06) |
| Number of Student-Year Observations | 949,446 | 946,729 |
| Number of Schools | 629 | 629 |

**TABLE B.4**

**Analysis of Whether Students Enrolled in Their Designated Welcoming School**

|  | Estimate | P-Value |
|---|---|---|
| Intercept | 0.199 | 0.6526 |
| **Student Characteristics** | | |
| Latino Student | 0.2878 | 0.0705 |
| White Student | 0.1901 | 0.5676 |
| Male Student | -0.0084 | 0.8686 |
| IEP Student | 0.1384 | 0.1543 |
| Free or Reduced-Price Lunch Student | 0.0103 | 0.9467 |
| Test Scores Unknown | 0.3714 | 0.1882 |
| Well Below-Average Test Scores | -0.0817 | 0.4246 |
| Below-Average Test Scores | -0.1169 | 0.2791 |
| Above-Average Test Scores | 0.0559 | 0.5610 |
| Well Above-Average Test Scores | -0.2272 | 0.0851 |
| Grade K | -0.0149 | 0.8732 |
| Grade 1 | -0.0316 | 0.7412 |
| Grade 3 | 0.4287 | 0.1181 |
| Grade 4 | 0.2449 | 0.3702 |
| Grade 5 | 0.3831 | 0.1389 |
| Grade 6 | 0.4383 | 0.1026 |
| Grade 7 | **0.6514** | **0.0172** |
| **Location and Residential Variables** | | |
| Lives in Attendance Area of Closed School | **0.2427** | **0.0059** |
| Changed Residence Summer 2012 | **-0.3808** | **0.0002** |
| Missing Data on Residential Moves | **-0.2813** | **0.0017** |
| Miles From Student's Residence to Welcoming School | **-0.1005** | **<0.0001** |
| **Neighborhood Characteristics** | | |
| Concentration of Poverty | 0.0313 | 0.5661 |
| Social Status | 0.1091 | 0.0712 |
| Crime Rate (log) | -0.0853 | 0.2358 |
| Number of Level 1 Schools within 1/2 mile of Student's Residence | **-0.1735** | **0.0463** |
| Number of Level 2 Schools within 1/2 mile of Student's Residence | **-0.1454** | **0.0325** |
| Number of Level 3 Schools within 1/2 mile of Student's Residence | -0.0476 | 0.4762 |
| Welcoming School Changed Location | **1.0795** | **<.0001** |
| On Prior Closing List | -0.0806 | 0.7491 |
| Difference School Performance Points (Welcoming – Closed) | **-0.0152** | **0.0128** |
| Level 1 Welcoming School | 0.3254 | 0.1567 |
| Level 3 Welcoming School | 0.4892 | 0.0526 |
| New Program Added to Welcoming School (such as STEM or IB program) | 0.0786 | 0.6258 |
| Transportation Offered to Welcoming School | **-0.5835** | **0.0245** |
| No Data on Safety Measure | 0.1247 | 0.7545 |
| Well Below-Average Level of Safety | -0.2437 | 0.2391 |
| Below-Average Level of Safety | -0.1745 | 0.4978 |
| Above-Average Level of Safety | **0.4662** | **0.0464** |
| Well Above-Average Level of Safety | **0.6516** | **0.0029** |

**Note:** Bold numbers indicate statistically significant results: $p<0.05$.

**Appendix B**

## Enrolling in Other CPS Schools

The sample of students for this analysis was based on the 3,464 students who reenrolled in a CPS school in the fall of 2013 other than the designated welcoming school. The analyses have been done on the differences in performance policy points, between designated welcoming school and the one attended (**first outcome in Table B.5**), between closed and the one attended (**the second outcome in Table B.5**), the probability of attending a Level 3 school (**the third outcome in Table B.5**) and finally the probability of attending a Level 1 school (**the last outcome in Table B.5**). For the first two outcomes we run linear models with the dependent variables being the differenced in performance policy points between two schools; the attended school minus the welcoming school in the first analysis, and the attended school minus the closed school in the second analysis. For the last two outcomes we run logistic models. In one case the dependent variable was coded as 1 when a student attended a Level 3 school, 0 otherwise. In the last set of analyses the dependent variable was coded as 1 when a student attended a Level 1 school, 0 otherwise. We included in each model variables about student characteristics, their neighborhood and the designated welcoming school. We clustered the standard errors on the 53 clusters formed by the closed schools and their respective designated welcoming schools (43 closed schools were assigned one welcoming school, two closed schools had two welcoming schools, and two closed schools had three welcoming schools assigned to them).

**TABLE B.5**

Analyses on Differences in Performance Policy Points and Performance Levels of Schools Attended If Not Designated Welcoming School

| | Different Outcomes | | | | | | | |
|---|---|---|---|---|---|---|---|---|
| | Difference Performance Policy Points "Attended-Welcoming" | | Difference Performance Policy Points "Attended-Closed" | | Attend Level 3 School (logistic regression) | | Attend Level 1 School (logistic regression) | |
| | Estimate | P-Value | Estimate | P-Value | Estimate | P-Value | Estimate | P-Value |
| Intercept | -8.59 | 0.13 | 16.00 | 0.09 | 0.03 | 0.96 | -1.75 | 0.02 |
| Latino Student | **5.02** | **0.03** | 3.56 | 0.36 | **-0.79** | **0.01** | 0.49 | 0.07 |
| White Student | 6.26 | 0.37 | 8.69 | 0.08 | **-13.37** | **<0.0001** | -0.17 | 0.79 |
| Male Student | 1.09 | 0.07 | 1.58 | 0.08 | **-0.15** | **0.040** | 0.09 | 0.30 |
| IEP Student | -0.13 | 0.95 | 0.60 | 0.82 | 0.17 | 0.35 | 0.14 | 0.59 |
| Free or Reduced-Price Lunch Student | 1.31 | 0.58 | -0.64 | 0.83 | -0.27 | 0.30 | -0.27 | 0.29 |
| Test Scores Unknown | 0.91 | 0.85 | -2.45 | 0.75 | 0.31 | 0.45 | 0.31 | 0.60 |
| Well Below-Average Test Scores | -2.47 | 0.10 | -2.57 | 0.11 | 0.26 | 0.12 | -0.20 | 0.33 |
| Below-Average Test Scores | -1.76 | 0.24 | -0.19 | 0.89 | 0.28 | 0.12 | -0.01 | 0.95 |
| Above-Average Test Scores | 0.70 | 0.69 | -0.13 | 0.95 | -0.10 | 0.62 | 0.27 | 0.27 |
| Well Above-Average Test Scores | 2.41 | 0.27 | -2.00 | 0.53 | -0.22 | 0.40 | -0.06 | 0.82 |
| Grade K | -1.35 | 0.32 | -1.39 | 0.34 | 0.18 | 0.22 | **-0.37** | **0.04** |
| Grade 1 | 1.10 | 0.37 | 0.90 | 0.44 | -0.01 | 0.96 | 0.03 | 0.85 |
| Grade 3 | 1.35 | 0.76 | -2.03 | 0.79 | 0.36 | 0.41 | 0.24 | 0.67 |
| Grade 4 | 1.67 | 0.71 | -4.02 | 0.61 | 0.02 | 0.97 | 0.14 | 0.81 |

**Note:** Bold numbers indicate statistically significant results: p<0.05.

**TABLE B.5:** *CONTINUED*

Analyses on Differences in Performance Policy Points and Performance Levels of Schools Attended If Not Designated Welcoming School

| | Different Outcomes | | | | | | | |
|---|---|---|---|---|---|---|---|---|
| | Difference Performance Policy Points "Attended-Welcoming" | | Difference Performance Policy Points "Attended-Closed" | | Attend Level 3 School | | Attend Level 1 School | |
| | Estimate | P-Value | Estimate | P-Value | Estimate | P-Value | Estimate | P-Value |
| Grade 5 | 2.07 | 0.65 | -2.55 | 0.75 | 0.17 | 0.70 | 0.34 | 0.57 |
| Grade 6 | 2.14 | 0.63 | -1.28 | 0.86 | 0.05 | 0.91 | 0.31 | 0.56 |
| Grade 7 | 0.44 | 0.92 | -4.76 | 0.52 | 0.27 | 0.51 | -0.11 | 0.84 |
| Concentration of Poverty in Neighborhood | -1.27 | 0.12 | -0.54 | 0.65 | 0.12 | 0.15 | -0.03 | 0.77 |
| Social Capital in Neighborhood | -0.02 | 0.97 | 0.22 | 0.81 | 0.02 | 0.85 | 0.05 | 0.62 |
| Attending Attendance Area School | 0.67 | 0.68 | -0.89 | 0.60 | -0.31 | 0.07 | -0.16 | 0.38 |
| Miles to Welcoming School from Residence | 0.66 | 0.11 | 0.30 | 0.55 | -0.06 | 0.11 | 0.04 | 0.49 |
| Level 1 Welcoming School | **-15.37** | **<.0001** | 2.90 | 0.64 | **-0.67** | **0.00** | 0.32 | 0.35 |
| Level 3 Welcoming School | **17.75** | **<.0001** | **8.75** | **0.04** | **-0.49** | **0.05** | **-0.54** | **0.03** |
| Number of Level 1 Schools within 1/2 Mile | **3.67** | **0.00** | **3.48** | **0.05** | **-0.23** | **0.00** | **0.95** | **<.0001** |
| Number of Level 2 Schools within 1/2 Mile | 0.72 | 0.25 | 0.70 | 0.56 | **-0.37** | **<.0001** | -0.14 | 0.13 |
| Number of Level 3 Schools within 1/2 Mile | **-3.94** | **<.0001** | **-2.36** | **0.04** | **0.53** | **<.0001** | -0.23 | 0.07 |
| Number of Observations | 3,274 | | 3,274 | | 3,327 | | 3,327 | |

**Note:** Bold numbers indicate statistically significant results: $p<0.05$.

# Appendix C
## Qualitative Sample and Analyses

## Sample

The primary purpose of the qualitative portion of our study was to understand why families enrolled in the schools they enrolled in and not others, and what constraints or barriers they faced during the process. Below is a detailed description of our sampling procedure.

### Sampling Closed Schools

First, we sampled closed schools for range using maximum heterogeneity sampling to capture a variety of parent perspectives.[38] In order to use maximum heterogeneity sampling effectively, we first identified the criteria for constructing our sample by examining five distinct clusters that emerged from the way CPS assigned designated welcoming schools to each closed school:

1. Closed schools with more than one designated welcoming school (10 percent of closed schools)

2. Closed schools with one designated welcoming school, but the attendance area boundaries of other schools were redrawn to include the attendance area boundary of the closed school (18 percent of closed schools)

3. Closed schools with one designated welcoming school, and only that one school had their attendance area redrawn (35 percent of closed schools)

4. Closed schools where the designated welcoming school moved location to the closed school building (35 percent of closed schools)

5. Closed schools with no attendance area, which includes special education schools and other specialized schools (2 percent of closed schools)

After arranging our sample of closed schools into the clusters identified above, we then examined the proportion of students from the closed schools who reenrolled the following fall in CPS schools, including: the designated welcoming school, other neighborhood schools, magnet schools, and charter schools. To get a range of perspectives, we chose some schools where the majority of students enrolled in the designated welcoming school, other schools where the majority of students enrolled in other CPS schools, and schools with a more even mix. In making the final selection of closed schools, we also took geographic location into consideration. Using a map of the city with community areas, we first determined which area the closed schools were located in and then made sure to select schools in different geographic locations so that we were not sampling only from one location in the city. In total, we sampled 12 closed schools: Two from cluster one; three from cluster two; five from cluster three; and two from cluster four. We also sampled a small percentage of families within cluster five.

### Sampling Displaced Families

We used a stratified, purposeful sampling procedure to sample families within our sample closed schools, based on a number of criteria. Similar to maximum heterogeneity sampling, the purpose of a stratified purposeful sampling procedure is to sample for variation (but variation based on predetermined stratified criteria). Because our major research question was about the choices and constraints families faced, we sampled families that enrolled in their designated welcoming schools as well as families that enrolled in other CPS neighborhood schools, magnet schools, or charter schools. In addition to these criteria, we also stratified families by grade level of children so that we talked to families with children in both early elementary grades (K-4) and middle grades (5-8). For families that enrolled their children into other CPS schools, we stratified our sample further into schools that were higher- and

---

**38** See Patton (2002) for more information on this type of sampling strategy.

**TABLE C.1**

Demographic Characteristics of Interviewees

| | Parents/ Guardians with Children Receiving Free or Reduced-Price Lunch (FRPL) | Parents/Guardians with Children Who have Individualized Education Programs (IEPs) | Parent/Guardian Race/Ethnicity | | | Total |
|---|---|---|---|---|---|---|
| | | | Black | Latino | Other | |
| All | 86 | 27 | 80 | 12 | 3 | 95 |
| Children Attended a Designated Welcoming School (DWS) | 45 | 14 | 43 | 5 | 2 | 50 |
| Children Attended a Lower-Rated School than the DWS or a School Not Rated | 26 | 9 | 23 | 5 | 0 | 28 |
| Children Attended a Higher-Rated School than the DWS | 15 | 4 | 14 | 2 | 1 | 17 |
| Children Attended a Lower-Rated School than the Closed School or a School Not Rated | 14 | 7 | 12 | 2 | 0 | 14 |
| Children Attended a Higher-Rated School than the Closed School | 27 | 6 | 25 | 5 | 1 | 31 |

lower-rated than their designated welcoming schools based on the district performance policy ratings. Lastly, we sampled at least one family that had a child with an IEP from each of the closed schools.

Within each of these stratifications, families were randomized and researchers called families until they reached approximately eight families for every sampled closed school. In total, we interviewed 95 families.

**Table C.1** shows the demographic characteristics of the parents/guardians we interviewed.

## Qualitative Analysis

Researchers designed an interview protocol to elicit answers from families about the kinds of information they received regarding their school choice options, the schools they were considering sending their children to and why, and why they ultimately decided to enroll their children in specific schools. We called families based on the sampling plan outlined above until we reached the number of families specified in each of the sampling categories (approximately eight families for each sampled closed school). Telephone interviews were conducted in June and July, 2014. On average, interviews lasted approximately 20 minutes. We audio recorded all telephone interviews and transcribed them verbatim. Researchers read each interview transcript multiple times and coded responses into appropriate question banks using Atlas.ti. Once interviews were organized by protocol question, researchers further coded interviews and extracted themes that emerged from the data. Data were organized in multiple ways, including Excel and Word tables to further examine patterns across the data.

## ABOUT THE AUTHORS

**MARISA DE LA TORRE** is the Director for Internal Research Capacity at UChicago CCSR. Two of her main research interests involve studying the effects of policies aimed at the lowest-performing schools in the district and the high school choice process in Chicago Public Schools. She is currently studying the impact that attending higher-performing high schools have on students' academic and nonacademic outcomes. Before joining UChicago CCSR, she worked for the Chicago Public Schools in the Office of Research, Evaluation, and Accountability. She received a master's degree in economics from Northwestern University.

**MOLLY F. GORDON** is a Senior Research Analyst at UChicago CCSR. Her current research focuses on the impact of closing schools on families, examining the 5 Essential Supports Surveys across Illinois, and investigating how school leadership influences instruction and student learning. Previously, she was a Research Associate at the Center for Applied Research and Educational Improvement (CAREI) at the University of Minnesota. She earned a BA in Philosophy and an MA in Educational Policy Studies from the University of Wisconsin–Madison, and a PhD in Educational Policy and Administration from the University of Minnesota–Twin Cities.

**PAUL MOORE** is a Research Analyst at UChicago CCSR and is in the process of completing an MA in the social sciences at the University of Chicago. His research interests include quantitative modeling and methodology. He is studying the effects of attending higher-performing schools on students' academic performance and noncognitive skills. He earned a BS in mathematics and education science from Vanderbilt University.

**JENNIFER COWHY** is a Research Analyst at UChicago CCSR. She received her master's degrees in social work and public policy from the University of Chicago and her BA in sociology from the University of Michigan. Her research interests include special education and supports in schools beyond the classroom. Her current research focuses on the impact of school closings on children and families and evaluations of education programs and policies.

*This report reflects the interpretation of the authors. Although UChicago CCSR's Steering Committee provided technical advice, no formal endorsement by these individuals, organizations, or the full Consortium should be assumed.*

# UCHICAGOCCSR

## CONSORTIUM ON CHICAGO SCHOOL RESEARCH

### Directors

**ELAINE M. ALLENSWORTH**
*Lewis-Sebring Director*

**EMILY KRONE**
*Director for Outreach and Communication*

**JENNY NAGAOKA**
*Deputy Director*

**MELISSA RODERICK**
*Senior Director*
*Hermon Dunlap Smith Professor*
*School of Social Service Administration*

**PENNY BENDER SEBRING**
*Founding Director*

**SUE SPORTE**
*Director for Research Operations*

**MARISA DE LA TORRE**
*Director for Internal Research Capacity*

### Steering Committee

**KATHLEEN ST. LOUIS CALIENTO**
Co-Chair
Spark, Chicago

**KIM ZALENT**
Co-Chair
Business and Professional People for the Public Interest

#### Ex-Officio Members

**TIMOTHY KNOWLES**
Urban Education Institute

#### Institutional Members

**JOHN R. BARKER**
Chicago Public Schools

**CLARICE BERRY**
Chicago Principals and Administrators Association

**AARTI DHUPELIA**
Chicago Public Schools

**CHRISTOPHER KOCH**
Illinois State Board of Education

**KAREN G.J. LEWIS**
Chicago Teachers Union

**SHERRY J. ULERY**
Chicago Public Schools

#### Individual Members

**VERONICA ANDERSON**
Communications Consultant

**JOANNA BROWN**
Logan Square Neighborhood Association

**CATHERINE DEUTSCH**
Illinois Network of Charter Schools

**RAQUEL FARMER-HINTON**
University of Wisconsin, Milwaukee

**KIRABO JACKSON**
Northwestern University

**CHRIS JONES**
Stephen T. Mather High School

**DENNIS LACEWELL**
Urban Prep Charter Academy for Young Men

**LILA LEFF**
Umoja Student Development Corporation

**RUANDA GARTH MCCULLOUGH**
Young Women's Leadership Academy

**LUISIANA MELÉNDEZ**
Erikson Institute

**CRISTINA PACIONE-ZAYAS**
Latino Policy Forum

**PAIGE PONDER**
One Million Degrees

**LUIS R. SORIA**
Chicago Public Schools

**BRIAN SPITTLE**
DePaul University

**MATTHEW STAGNER**
Mathematica Policy Research

**AMY TREADWELL**
Chicago New Teacher Center

**ERIN UNANDER**
Al Raby High School

**ARIE J. VAN DER PLOEG**
American Institutes for Research (Retired)

www.ingramcontent.com/pod-product-compliance
Lightning Source LLC
Chambersburg PA
CBHW060821090426

42738CB00002B/63